PAShNiT . com

How To Ride a
MOTORCYCLE

A Rider's Guide to Strategy, Safety, and Skill Development

Pat Hahn
Photography by Evans Brasfield

MOTORBOOKS

ACKNOWLEDGMENTS

I am grateful most of all to my wife Kristin and my family. Their love and support help me become the motorcyclist, writer, and person I hope to be.

Heartfelt thanks to my good friends John Gateley and Darwin Holmstrom, whose encouragement, advice, and B.S.-detectors made this book what it is.

Hats off to Andy Goldfine and the crew at the Rider Wearhouse: brilliant creations, great service and support, and true enthusiasm.

And thanks, as always, to my various muses: the enthusiasts of Minnesota Sportbike, the Central Roadracing Association, the hedonists of Team Poop, the Motorcycle Safety Foundation, Keith Code, Kent Larson, Karl Rehpohl, Brent Jass, and Jeff Giacomini, who started this whole ball rolling in 1990 by landing on his head.

First published in 2005 by Motorbooks, an imprint of MBI Publishing Company, Galtier Plaza, Suite 200, 380 Jackson Street, St. Paul, MN 55101-3885 USA

© Pat Hahn, 2005
All photography by Evans Brasfield unless otherwise noted

Motorbooks titles are also available at discounts in bulk quantity for industrial or sales-promotional use. For details write to Special Sales Manager at MBI Publishing Company, Galtier Plaza, Suite 200, 380 Jackson Street, St. Paul, MN 55101-3885 USA.

ISBN-13: 978-0-7603-2114-0
ISBN-10: 0-7603-2114-0

On the front cover: Kawasaki Ninja 500R. *Kevin Wing*

On the frontispiece: Use it if you must, avoid it if you can. The high speeds of the freeway combined with the poor perception and skills of typical drivers can create a motorcycle-eating machine. The side roads are much more fun.

On the title page: Half of all motorcycle fatalities happen on roads just like this one. Don't get too overconfident when your only distractions are blue sky and fresh air.

On the back cover, left: Self-evaluation is great for any rider, but little compares to the informed and honest feedback from a co-rider on riding style and technique.
Right: While you're learning, it's easiest to shift at certain points on the speedometer. After several hours of practice, you'll start to shift based on the way the engine sounds. When that happens, you will have just made another leap in your evolution as a motorcyclist.

Editor: Peter Schletty
Designer: Kari Johnston

Printed in China

CONTENTS

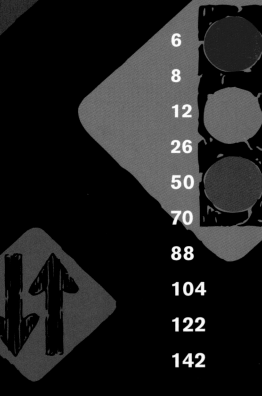

FOREWORD

A few years back I wrote a book called *The Complete Idiot's Guide to Motorcycles* which contained a section on how to ride a motorcycle. Because that was just one section in a very large book, it only covered riding basics in the broadest strokes possible. I found this to be a necessary evil when trying to cram information on every aspect of motorcycling into one volume. When I wrote the section on how to ride a motorcycle, I generally deferred to accepted Motorcycle Safety Foundation practices and directed readers to take the MSF riding courses at their earliest opportunity. I wanted to provide more detail, but I consoled myself that if the information in the book saved just one life, if just one rider took an MSF course and started wearing proper safety gear, it would be worth the effort.

Still, the fact that the book didn't contain riding instruction in further detail, that it didn't take the reader beyond those first shaky trips around his or her neighborhood, bothered me. I felt that the motorcycling community needed something more.

A couple of years after writing the first edition of that book I met Mr. Patrick Hahn, a young man so enthusiastic about motorcycle safety that he had made a career out of the topic. Enthusiasm is well and good, but Pat had something even more important—the ability to express his ideas in entertaining and accessible ways. I found that listening to Pat explain riding concepts made me a better and safer rider. At the time I met Pat I'd been riding for over 25 years, yet here I was, an old dog learning new tricks. Not only did I learn new tricks, but I also gained a better understanding of the old ones I'd been using instinctively for decades.

Our long discussions on the topic eventually led to Pat writing his first book, *Ride Hard, Ride Smart*. Editing that book changed my entire approach to riding a motorcycle. It even changed my approach to driving a car. I may have saved a few lives when I wrote my book, but Pat Hahn saved a lot of lives with *Ride Hard, Ride Smart*.

I believe he will save even more lives with the book you hold in your hands. *How to Ride a Motorcycle* will become the essential tool for beginning motorcyclists, one recommended by riding instructors around the world. Like my *Idiot's Guide*, Pat strongly stresses the importance of taking an MSF class. There is, after all, no substitute for hands-on, one-on-one training from a flesh-and-blood riding coach or for the kind of feedback you receive from fellow human beings. But likewise there is no substitute for the information available in this book. *How to Ride a Motorcycle* provides information that is not available anywhere else.

A key factor in making *How to Ride a Motorcycle* so invaluable is that it provides the information you'll need to go beyond those first few wobbly rides. In these pages Pat guides you along your journey from the parking lot to city streets to county roads to the super slab. This doesn't end with the weekend course in the parking lot of a community college; *How to Ride a Motorcycle* provides lessons for the entire first year of riding. Think of it as a riding instructor that goes home with you. Pat knows his stuff. He knows the risks you'll face and the obstacles you'll have to overcome during your first season, and he's written

a book to help shepherd a new rider through that critical time period. This is a graduated lesson plan, beginning with the acquisition of a rider's first motorcycle and ending with that rider becoming a skilled and safe motorcyclist.

Like an MSF riding course and a quality helmet, a new rider should consider this book an essential part of his or her riding kit. Pat's writing talent and good humor make this an especially enjoyable part of that kit. Buy the book, use it, and if you ever see Mr. Hahn in person, if you see him at a book signing or motorcycle event, please take the opportunity to introduce yourself. You'll find he's as enjoyable in the flesh as he is on paper.

—Darwin Holmstrom
Crystal, Minnesota
June, 2005

Darwin Holmstrom is the author or co-author of five books on motorcycling, including The Complete Idiot's Guide to Motorcycles, BMW Motorcycles, *and* Billy Lane Chop Fiction: It's not a Motorcycle, Baby; It's a Chopper.

INTRODUCTION

If you want to ride a motorcycle, the most important thing you can do is to be smart about it.

What does it mean to be smart about motorcycling? Riding smart means knowing exactly what you're getting into, knowing what you're doing when you're out there, and taking what you're doing seriously. Knowledge and attitude—not necessarily skill—are what separate real motorcyclists from fake ones.

What's a Poser?
Fake riders, or "posers," decide they want to look like riders, and that's where their interest in motorcycling ends. There's nothing intelligent about it. A poser thinks the motorcycle completes his or her image and spends as much money as necessary in order to look the part. Most of the time, you can tell the difference between motorcycle riders and motorcycle posers by their odometer or how clean their riding gear is, but not always. Posers do things like rub dirt or scratches into their jackets or knee pucks to make it look like they've seen some miles. Or they haul their motorcycles 500 miles on a trailer but pull the bikes out for the last 30 so they can look and feel like they *rode* there.

A motorcycle *rider*, on the other hand, digs deep into riding, discovers that part of him or herself that is the motorcyclist they want to be, and spends the rest of his or her free time trying to release that prisoner. Life for a motorcyclist is a battle between work and play, between responsibility and self-indulgent hedonism, trying to bring that socially shackled motorcyclist to the surface and enjoy and the freedom of the road. Motorcyclists work hard to be smart about their riding, always craving more knowledge, always craving more experience. Let's just call them "enthusiastic."

True, devoted motorcyclists (enthusiasts) and posers can sometimes be difficult to tell apart. The differences aren't always obvious to the innocent bystander. But by the time you finish reading this book, you will be able to tell the real from the fake, because you'll be on your way to becoming a real motorcycle rider.

In the beginner's mind there are many possibilities, in the expert's mind, few.
—Hindu proverb

What you see on the street seems simple enough: a guy on a bike. But what you don't see are the training, the years of experience, and the many levels of knowledge that make it even possible for him to be there, let alone the attitude that rider needs to survive.

Why Would I Care?

The problem with posers is that they rarely do anything (aside from spending money) to make motorcycling better. All they do is drive up the price of our bikes and our insurance rates, not to mention injury and fatality statistics. They are, however, keeping the chrome polish, leather, and expensive sunglasses manufacturers in business.

What I hope to achieve by writing this book—and by you reading it—is to point you in the right direction so you learn to ride and contribute to motorcycling in a positive way. I want you to discover and share the joy of motorcycling with everyone you know. I want your enthusiasm to resonate with your family, your friends, your neighbors, and your coworkers. I want you to help in the big push to make motorcycling a more accepted and appreciated social good.

A Titanic Analogy

What you most need to understand at this point in your journey is that there is a lot more to motorcycling than just what you see at the surface.

A poser is the equivalent of a tourist. Tourists on cruise ships only get to see the little nub at the top of the iceberg floating just above the surface, plainly visible, and take lots of mental pictures. To their eyes, it's as big as a mountain. The tourist thinks, "So that's an iceberg. Wow. Impressive." They say this, though sometimes not really knowing why, being impressed because they believe they should be impressed, maybe, and saying so because that's what you're supposed to say when you see something impressive.

Posers are the same way and think, "Motorcycle = cool." They're impressed with what they see, and satisfied in the knowledge that there's nothing more they need to know.

But the true drama of an iceberg is what lies beneath. What you can't see could sink a ship! With icebergs, as well as motorcycling, it's not obvious how much more there is

The true drama of an iceberg—and motorcycling—is what lies beneath.

Tourists (and posers) are satisfied with what's visible on the surface. But enthusiasts know there's more to it than that. When you see a motorcyclist on the road, this is all you see—the tip of the iceberg. Real enthusiasts know what lies beneath, and what it takes to get there. John Gateley

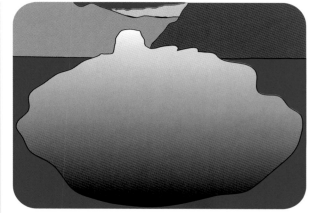

What you can see on the surface is plainly visible, and if you're lucky, you might catch the faintest glimpse of what's just barely beneath the surface—what you can see through the water. But beware: as you go deeper, it gets darker, murkier, and the view becomes less clear. You know it's down there; it's just harder to see.

On the street you see only the outward characteristics of a motorcyclist. You're missing the attitudes, training, information, formative experiences, knowledge, skills, and enthusiasm that transformed a person from a workaday transportationist to a roadhugging motorcycle hedonist—someone who can no longer think of going anywhere without considering the motorcycle as the most rational option. How's that for freedom of the road?

I'm going to attempt to take the mystery out of what lies beneath the surface of a motorcyclist. Starting with what you can see, we're going to dig deep into what makes it happen.

Chapter 1
Chapter 2
Chapter 3
Chapter 4
Chapter 5
Chapter 6
Chapter 7

to it without good information and some education. What a tourist can see floating above the surface is just a fraction of the enormous mass of ice that keeps that little frozen hat on top of the water. And what a motorist, nonrider, or poser can't see in your average, everyday motorcyclist is what lies beneath. There's a lot more to it than meets the eye. Smart riders know this. Posers don't.

On the street you see only the outward characteristics of a motorcyclist. You're missing the attitudes, training, information, formative experiences, knowledge, skills, and enthusiasm that transformed a person from a workaday transportationist to a roadhugging motorcycle hedonist— someone who can no longer think of going anywhere without considering the motorcycle as the most rational option. How's that for freedom of the road?

A smart rider understands that there's always more to motorcycling and that you're never done learning.

How to Use This Book
Herein you'll find the smartest basic approach to becoming a motorcyclist, the steps you'll take to get there, and tips to help you think your way around the corners of problems as you learn. I'm going to give you tools to evaluate yourself and your riding ability along the way, so you know where you are and where you're going next.

You'll also get good insider information—Big Secrets One through Seven are hard to come by on your own— so that you don't have to learn everything the hard way. I'll try to dispel some common myths about motorcycling in special sections titled, "What People Say and What People Mean." These will help you avoid the trap of blaming someone or something else when things don't go your way. And they'll also give me a chance to poke fun at some of the silly things that people say to hide their ignorance.

You'll also find something here that's never been seen before: strategies and focused drills for new riders to use while learning on the street. The concepts and exercises in this book will bridge the gap from MSF course graduate to skilled, competent rider. If you're looking for advice to survive your first six months on a bike while learning the ropes, you've found it.

Read through the entire book first so you get the big picture. Once you have an idea of what you're in for, then come back and study specific chapters while you're in that phase. This book will mirror the stages of your riding "career." The chapters are designed as a guide so you know what to expect, what to do next, and when you're ready to move on. The book will read quickly. Expect the real thing to take some time. While this book might only take you a few days to read, becoming a motorcyclist will take many years.

There's a *lot* more to riding a motorcycle than what you'll find here, so I'll tell you right now that you cannot rely on this book alone. So, at the end of each chapter you'll find recommended magazines, books, and Web sites appropriate for that stage of your riding career. This book has everything you need to get started and a "road map" guide for your development as a rider, but you can't get it all from just one book. Besides, you'll want to absorb multiple viewpoints to devise your own riding philosophy anyway. Take in as much information as you can along the way so you'll be a well-read, well-informed motorcyclist.

(If this all sounds like too much work and you'd rather just be a poser, you can skip Chapters 1, 2, 4, 5, 6, and 7. Just read Chapter 3 and get it over with. Go have fun and look cool, and try not to get yourself killed. And thanks for buying my book.)

Take care not to rush things or grow impatient with your skill progression. Becoming skilled at anything takes time, and in no case is it more true than motorcycling. There's an old saying that goes something like, "A true traveler has no set schedule and is not intent on getting there." Let that be your first and overarching attitude toward motorcycling. Enjoy the journey, relish the little victories along the way, and most of all, have fun.

Becoming skilled at anything takes time, and in no case is it more true than motorcycling.

About the Author

Pat Hahn is a motorcycle safety instructor ("rider coach"), motorcycle public information and education coordinator for the Minnesota Motorcycle Safety Center, and author of the advanced riding strategies book *Ride Hard, Ride Smart*. He uses his bike to commute to work, run errands, entertain friends, burn off steam on twisty roads on the weekends, take long trips around the country, and teach others how to make the most of their own bikes and skills. Pat lives with his wife Kristin and other fuzzier family members in south Minneapolis.

An amateur roadracer, Pat conducts advanced cornering and safety seminars for sportbike enthusiasts and has contributed to other books, such as Evans Brasfield's *101 Sportbike Performance Projects* and Kent Larson's *Motorcycle Track Day Handbook*. He learned to ride the hard way—on his own, on a bike way too big and powerful for him, without a helmet, in downtown Chicago—fifteen years ago, and has since worked tirelessly to hone his skills into a simple all-inclusive strategy. He's learned quite a few tricks that will help you get started, ride safely, and grow into a serious, educated motorcyclist.

GETTING PREPARED

UST AS THERE'S A LOT MORE TO MOTORCYCLING THAN MEETS THE EYE, THERE'S A LOT TO KNOW BEFORE YOU EVEN GET STARTED. YOU CAN'T JUST THROW A LEG OVER AND GO.

Motorcycle riders are a different breed. They've chosen a mode of transportation, a type of recreation, and a time-consuming (sometimes all-consuming) passion that most "normal" people think is nuts. In a way, motorcyclists are nuts—they're born with the same eyes and hands and feet as everyone else, but somehow they decide that the best way to use them is to ride around on a machine that, with one false move, can hurl them headfirst to their doom. They've decided to forego the relative safety and surety of a four-wheeled vehicle and master one that requires balance, skill, training, and strategy—all that just to keep it from falling over in the driveway—and then head out into traffic on it.

So are motorcycle riders so different from other types of drivers? Yes. It's their motivation, attitude toward driving, and assessment of the risks they face that makes them so.

The fun and the challenge of motorcycling are what draw most enthusiasts to the road. If you're staring at this photo like a dog stares at the last pork chop, you've come to the right place. Read on.

Some people prefer to soak in the tub, but motorcyclists prefer to leave it all behind and get reacquainted with their world. If it's solitude you crave, a motorcycle is a willing (and thankfully untalkative) accomplice. H. Peuker courtesy KTM

Instead of watching the world go by through a car's windshield as if you're watching TV, when you ride you're on the television, tasting every part of the landscape with your five senses and putting on a terrific show for your viewers.

Self-Evaluation

A rider's most important skill, more important than any training, technique, or strategy, is that of self-awareness. Being on a first-name basis with your mind, your body, your experience, your attitudes, and your emotions will help you understand your limitations. On a motorcycle, when you overstep your limitations, you crash, so it's critical to evaluate yourself every time you ride, and every step of the way. A human being is never the same person twice. He or she is constantly changing, sometimes for better, sometimes for worse. Knowing who you are and of what you're capable at any given moment will help you keep your riding under control.

But for starters, you need to ask yourself: "Why do I want to ride a motorcycle?" And be honest. No matter what your reasoning, it's great that you want to learn to ride, but you need to take a close look at your motivation in order to understand the challenges you'll face along the way.

Understanding Motorcyclist Motivation

There are probably as many reasons for wanting to ride a motorcycle as there are motorcyclists, but there are a few that many people have in common:

Fun. Motorcycles are an absolute blast to ride. They're fast, they sound great, and they take to corners and the open road like a hound dog to a bunny rabbit. The sun is warmer, the breeze cooler, the ocean air saltier, and the autumn leaves more fragrant when you're on a bike. Instead of watching the world go by through a car's windshield as if you're watching TV, when you ride you're *on* the television, tasting every part of the landscape with your five senses and putting on a terrific show for your viewers.

Challenge. Motorcycles are tricky to operate and even trickier to operate skillfully. A rider uses every appendage he or she has to work all the controls on a bike—head, eyes, shoulders, elbows,

Riders often happily find themselves with easy parking, because they can use spaces no other vehicle can.

While it can be frustrating at first, one of the many joys of riding is the satisfaction of mastering a powerful throbbing hunk of heavy beautiful machinery.

arms, hands, thumbs, butt, legs, knees, feet—with precision and control. While it can be frustrating at first, one of the many joys of riding is the satisfaction of mastering a powerful throbbing hunk of heavy beautiful machinery. The psychological reward of taking on traffic with a machine that leaves your "cheese in the wind" and making it home safely is a thrill many riders can't live without.

Advantage. Being smaller, lighter, and more nimble than most four-wheelers gives motorcycles an edge in traffic. No, scratch that. Being smaller, lighter, and nimbler than most four-wheelers gives motorcycles a *huge* edge in traffic. Generally, any bike can outaccelerate, outbrake, outcorner, and outshine any typical passenger vehicle. Even better, in more open-minded jurisdictions, things

like lane splitting and filtering are not only allowed, but encouraged.

Isolation. Motorcycling is, by nature, a solitary activity. When you hop on your motorcycle you immerse yourself in the outdoors and cut yourself off from everyone simultaneously. You get to go out and breathe in your world without having to put up with all the B.S. that sometimes goes along with it. It's easy to forget your worries and spend some quality time with yourself on a bike because you don't have things like e-mail, ringing telephones, barking dogs, screaming kids, or needy relatives clogging your psychological "in" basket with anything nonmotorcycle.

Beware though: This treasured isolation is only a sure bet while you're moving. Motorcycles and motorcycling

Lane Splitting: In states that allow it, riding between lanes of slow or stopped traffic, easing congestion on crowded highways.

Filtering: Mostly seen in Europe and Asia, motorcycles and scooters squeeze between and in front of vehicles, essentially "cutting in" to the front of the line at a stoplight. Smaller size and superior acceleration allow the bikes to pull away quickly, easing congestion in crowded urban areas.

are conversation starters whether you like it or not. The guy at the gas station, that oddball rider on the old red BMW who seemed quiet when he asked if he could ride with you, he might just talk your ear off at the next gas stop. . . .

Economy. Let's face it, motorcycles can be cheap compared to cars. The purchase price is lower, gas mileage is better, insurance is cheaper (usually), exhaust emissions fewer, they require less work, and cost less to park, maintain, and clean. And with a nod toward fun, you can get the performance and handling of a $60,000 sports car for about $10,000, and if you wreck it you'll have enough money left for five more!

Friends. Ironically, while motorcycling is essentially a solitary act, lots of people get into it because they have friends who ride. By jumping in they step into a new world of fun, camaraderie, sport, travel, skill, and knowledge. Riding offers a new way to explore the countryside, whether that's close to home or half a continent away, with good friends and those not yet met. And unlike car drivers, when a rider sees another rider broken down on the side of the road, it's a good bet they'll stop and offer help.

Looks. Arguably the dumbest reason to ride a motorcycle, but the fact is a rider, mysterious underneath a black helmet with a smoked face shield, wearing form-fitting leather, putting a muscular machine through its paces in an environment as challenging as twenty-first century traffic, is *sexy.* There's a reason all bikers seem to dress alike and look alike—they've found the winning combination of accoutrements to find and attract members of the opposite sex. Motorcycle + leather + sunglasses + various snaps, buttons, zippers, and chains = find mate. Even if your objective isn't romance or species propagation, all the people in your neighborhood will wave at you when you ride by, all your nieces and nephews will think you're really cool, and all your coworkers and relatives will think you're dangerous—especially when they're trapped in an elevator with you and you're covered with bugs from the weekend's ride.

Unlike car drivers, when a rider sees another rider broken down on the side of the road, it's a good bet they'll stop and offer help.

Motorcyclists are different from everyone else. What makes them do what they do, wear what they wear, and think like they think? Are they really so different? (Special thanks to Ben Fruehauf and Karl Rehpohl, and yes, ladies, they're both single.)

If you're looking for a mate, look no further. Here he is, stronger and more virile than any man on earth, able to control the wild beast that is his motorcycle while thumbing his nose at The Man and threatening all the lesser males within his territory. (If you want to look like a biker, that's great. But if attracting the opposite sex is the only reason you want to ride a motorcycle, just buy the outfit and leave the bike for someone who has an interest in riding, okay?)
Photo by Mark Langello

Motorcycles are challenging, but those challenges can overwhelm you and send you barreling headlong into the grille of an oncoming Mack truck.

Bad Motivation! Bad!

While all the above are reason enough to ride, they also have equally negative sides.

While motorcycles are fun, you can easily get carried away and in the blink of an eye find yourself wadded up against a tree with your back broken, blood trickling out of your ears, and no one around for miles.

While motorcycles are challenging, those challenges can overwhelm you and send you barreling headlong into the grille of an oncoming Mack truck.

While motorcycles have an advantage over cars in the performance department, they're also inherently unstable, have limited traction, and leave the rider extremely vulnerable in the event of an unplanned dismount.

While isolation is a reward in and of itself, it can also mean you find yourself stranded in the middle of nowhere with a broken bike or a broken leg or a broken head and no witnesses besides the deer that surprised you before deciding to take the long way 'round. While a motorcycle's economy is great, certain drivers with certain bikes will find that they're suddenly uninsurable, tires are expensive and have only a fraction of the life of car tires, plastic bodywork costs a small fortune to replace, and the tiny steel mystery box that sends all those ponies to the rear wheel can be very expensive to fix.

While friends can make motorcycling better, they can also get you into a lot of trouble trying to keep pace with them (or impress them!) before you've reached that level of skill.

And looks? Well, if your motivation is to "look" like a motorcycle rider and none of these other reasons appeal to you, then you should just buy the costume and skip the bike—your fascination with the way you look will one day undermine your ability to back

Big Secret Number 1:
The Never-Ending Roller Coaster

"If I had to explain, you wouldn't understand." Phooey. It's really simple, and almost anybody can understand it, whether they need it explained or not.

A carnival or amusement park is filled with what we nostalgically call "thrill rides." And probably the greatest, most universally accepted thrill ride we can imagine is a roller coaster. It rides on rails and goes exactly where it's supposed to, climbs to dizzying heights, plunges earthward at breakneck speeds, squashes you into the seat, and sends g-forces rushing through your body. It corners exactly as it's meant to corner, and all the time you're barely strapped in, feeling like you could be flung into outer space at any moment. The terror, the vulnerability, and the sensations are the thrill.

This is motorcycling, except motorcycling is 10 times better. On a bike, you actually get to steer the roller coaster and you never have to wait in line to get on and ride. You control the speed, you can ride as long as you want, and you only have to get off when you're tired or hungry. The terror is something you deal with every day; you learn to manage it, manipulate it, and beat it at its own game. And this roller coaster goes exactly where you want it—to faraway places, through incredible scenery, or simply to work in the morning and home at night.

Imagine the look on your face (and your heart rate!) if you rode a roller coaster to work every day.

These things cost millions and everybody has to share. A motorcycle costs less than a cheap car, and you don't have to share with anybody.

Imagine the look on your face (and your heart rate!) if you rode a roller coaster to work every day.

it up with skill, and you'll find yourself sliding on your face, hands, and chest into a steel guardrail. You won't look very pretty when it's all over.

I don't mean to scare potential riders with all the deathtalk here, but it's important to see both sides of the picture clearly so you can know exactly *why* you want to ride, what you want to get out of it, and the risks, obstacles, and pitfalls you should expect to encounter along the way.

There's only one person in this photo who is more likely to die or be injured in an accident. Is it going to matter whose fault the crash is, if someone's life changes because of it?

In the big scheme of things, whenever anything goes wrong on the road, it's the rider who suffers the consequences.

A Rider State of Mind

Motorcycle riders, if they want to survive, have to abandon their old notions of what it means to drive, and they have to learn new ones. Most people don't think too much about driving. Potential motorcyclists, interested in exploring a new way to use the roads, tend to be driving enthusiasts who care about skill, courtesy, and the thrill of a well-wrung machine. These people are already better at driving than average. Motorcycle riders are yet a step above—driving enthusiasts with an understanding of their extreme vulnerability in traffic and a very, very different way of looking at driving.

I should warn you, you may disagree with the following three theories. That's *good*. You *should* disagree—in your heart. (These theories are, admittedly, Nattering Nabobs of Negativism—repeat them too loudly and even your best riding friends will smack you. You'll be the babbling quicksand on Buzzkill Island that everyone avoids.) You don't have to agree with these theories, but you do have to pretend you do. Adopt them as guidelines. Act as if you believe them, and they will make all the difference in your riding career.

Nattering Nabobs of Negativism: Those people who will always tell you you're making a mistake. Smile appreciatively, take it all in, and then prove 'em wrong.

Attitude Number 1: Motorcyclists are responsible for everything that happens on the road. Not only is a rider responsible for his or her own safety (gear, skills, and strategy), a rider is also responsible for everyone else's actions and every*thing* else as well. Forget about riding around in an SUV, in which if you make a mistake it's a matter of trading insurance information or calling a tow truck and heading off on your merry little way. If you make a mistake on a motorcycle your day—or your life—is pretty much over.

In the big scheme of things, whenever anything goes wrong on the road, it's the rider who suffers the consequences. It doesn't matter whose fault it is or who had the right of way. If a car leaps out in front of a motorcycle in an intersection, the motorcycle is going to lose. Curve too tight? Rider's fault. (Should've slowed

Ride as if every other person on the road is trying to kill you. Thankfully, they're not, but riding as if this were true will allow you to find places on the road where absolutely no one can touch you—even if they wanted to.

more.) Dog ran out into the road? Rider's fault. (Should have seen the dog earlier and stopped.) Car pulled out in front of you? Rider's fault. (Should have expected it and taken evasive action.) Train fell off a bridge trestle and crushed the rider? Rider's fault. (Rider chose to be on his or her motorcycle that day.) Any rider with an aversion to expensive repairs, pain, and missing body parts has to take the world onto his or her shoulders.

(This is not to imply that everything is the rider's fault! There's a "legal" way to look at it and a "safe" way to look at it. What I'm saying here is that this is the *attitude* riders should take in order to survive in the big traffic game. There are courtrooms and armchairs from which to sort out just who is liable for what. But if you'd rather be out riding than stuck in a courtroom with a pair of broken wrists, collarbones, and thumbs, best make an attitude check. Being ultraparanoid can make your life much, much easier.)

Attitude Number 2: All other drivers are deliberately trying to kill you. They're not merely arrogant yuppies or brain-dead zombies who can fog a mirror and get their driver's license. Their goal is to run you over, smash into you, run you off the road, or otherwise find a way to wreck your day. Your job, on the other hand, is to make sure they can't touch you.

Deviant: A driver who's doing something different than everybody else.

Other drivers are wild cards, unpredictable and totally random in their little man-made world of seatbelts, air conditioning, and cruise control. The best you can do is expect the Other Guy to make the worst possible decision at the worst possible time—and try not to be there when it happens. Expect the worst and hope for the best, so all of your surprises are happy surprises.

Attitude Number 3: The road is designed to make you crash. Let's face it, the only "safe" road would be one that went dead straight and had no hills, intersections, or other vehicles. And even then a rider with poor skills or poor judgment would crash. Add weather, sand, oil spills, sharp turns, four-way stops, on-ramps, deer, drunk drivers, bicyclists, commuters on

cell phones, yellow lights, and the occasional "freeway couch," and you have a melting pot of hazards that are all converging on you and your motorcycle to send you into the next world.

Changing Your Mind

Consider, too, the transition every rider must make when switching from a four-wheel mindset to two-wheel mindset. It's not difficult to accommodate it when you're learning (because you *know* you don't know how to ride yet), but it's particularly insidious for experienced riders who don't ride every day. These people *think* they know it all, when the reality is, they've forgotten most of it.

You probably learned to drive in a relatively large vehicle that didn't require the balance and skill a motorcycle does. You've grown accustomed to dealing with the road and traffic from the relative safety of a steel cage with bumpers, an impact-absorbing frame, seatbelts, and air bags. You've gotten used to the insulation from the elements that a car or SUV provides, and most likely have been involved in some sort of accident from which you walked away with minor injuries—if any. You've probably also gotten a little lazy: talked on the phone, switched CDs, or fumbled with fast food while driving. Maybe even drinking before driving. All these factors make your brain and survival instinct numb to the reality of riding a motorcycle—the smallest mistake can get you killed.

What's worse, once you become a motorcyclist, every time you drive a car you fall right back into that mindset and have to start over from scratch every time you ride again. This is one of the biggest problems recreational riders face, and few of them, if any, ever realize it. Every time you're on the road in a vehicle other than your motorcycle, you start erasing the

One of the greatest side effects of learning to ride is that it makes you a better car driver. You'll be more conscious of other drivers and attuned to personal space, following distance, and hazard perception.

Weekend warriors are fooling themselves. They spend all week driving around in their two-ton steel cages and carry that mindset with them when they hop on their bikes for a Saturday evening ride. Smart riders understand that they can't just jump right in. They either give themselves more time and space to get reacquainted, or they sell the car and ride full-time so they don't have to make this very dangerous transition.
Photo by Mark Langello

Most motorcyclists would agree that riding a motorcycle actually makes you a better car driver, especially when dealing with other traffic. Unfortunately, it doesn't work the other way. The more time you spend in a car, the more you erode your motorcycle skills. Even when you're in a car, think like a motorcyclist to stay sharp.

mental skills you've worked so hard to build. This is why so many of the riders killed and injured are the ones who only ride for fun, once in a while.

It's important to note, though, that this can work both ways. You don't actually start at "ground zero" on your bike after you drive a car; you just need more time to get into the swing of things. The more often you drive a car, the more time you'll need. Also, you don't immediately revert back to a mindless SUV deviant every time you step off your bike—far from it. One of the greatest side effects of learning to ride is that it makes you a better car driver. You'll be more conscious of other drivers and attuned to personal space, following distance, and hazard perception.

Three Degrees of Separation 101

Three primary things separate motorcycle riders from car drivers: their clothing, their skills, and their strategy.

Motorcycle riding gear is the most obvious of the three and serves two purposes: comfort and protection. At first you might think all that gear makes you look like a dork, but the fact is that a rider isn't blessed with the safety and isolation from the elements that car drivers get. Heat, cold, wind, rain, and flying debris like dust, bugs, birds, and road alligators all work together to make riding miserable and dangerous. Good motorcycle gear is designed to minimize the negative effects of weather and flying objects, which in turn allows you to concentrate on what's really important: having fun and riding well.

(Road) Alligator: That snake-looking thing that you see lying in the middle of your lane, a tread from a semi tire.

What's more, as a motorcyclist you've got your knees in the breeze, and when things go wrong and you find yourself suddenly and irrevocably separated from your motorcycle, what you're wearing is all you have left between you and the ground. Protective riding gear is made of materials that absorb impacts and abrasions while you're slipping, sliding, bouncing, and tumbling down the road, wondering what in the hell just happened and where exactly your bike is.

Three primary things separate motorcycle riders from car drivers: Their clothing, their skills, and their strategy.

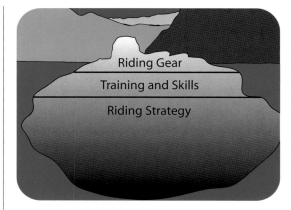

The three things that separate motorcycle riders from everyone else, from the most obvious to the least obvious: gear, skills, and brain. But from the most important to the least important it's brain, skills, and gear. Riding strategy creates the foundation and holds everything together, riding skills are piled on top of that to create a formidable defense, and riding gear tops it all off to create one simple, unified system.

The subtlest trait that separates motorcycle riders from car drivers is their overall approach to the road— their riding strategy.

Next on the list are the specialized skills a rider needs to control the bike. It seems any idiot who can fog a mirror can get a driver's license, but it takes special training and skills to earn a motorcycle endorsement, and a whole lot of practice and preparation to put it to use when it counts.

In addition to mastering timing and inputs to the various levers, twistgrips, pedals, and switches, motorcyclists also have to deal closely with the realities of gravity, balance, gyroscopic effect, centripetal force, inertia, traction management, weight bias, road camber, and countersteering—all in addition to keeping an eye out for everyone else on the road. Holy crap, that's a lot of responsibility. While it might look simple enough to a tourist or a poser, there's a lot more to it than just throwing a leg over and hitting the road—and it takes a long time to understand how it all fits together.

Gravity, balance, gyroscopic effect, centripetal force, inertia, traction management, weight bias, road camber, and countersteering: Read on. It'll all become clear by the end.

The subtlest trait that separates motorcycle riders from car drivers is their overall approach to the road—their riding strategy. Accepting the vulnerability of a motorcycle means always planning for the worst. In any mishap, the motorcycle is the most likely vehicle to lose control, and the rider is the most likely to lose body parts, so the motorcyclist has to work constantly at staying out of harm's way.

This means that riders need to try to control their environment. A skilled rider can read the road and the traffic well in advance, know everything that's going on around him, and position himself carefully to allow as much space as possible.

To survive for any length of time on a motorcycle, you literally need to read minds. You need enough knowledge, experience, and imagination to know what stupid thing some idiot driver is going to do ten seconds before they do it, and take steps to either make sure it doesn't happen or get yourself out of the way. Your goal is to minimize the number of surprises you encounter on the road.

Developing a superior riding strategy is the simplest, cheapest, and funnest way to smack the curve balls riding throws at you out of the park every time. (Overcoming the challenge of those curve balls themselves makes for a rollicking good time.) In theory, a good strategy can protect you from everything that could possibly go wrong.

But the real world doesn't work like that, and one in ten of those curve balls is going to leave a mark—probably right on your temple. That's where your riding skills step in. When the one clever hazard slips past your mental defense, your hands and body take over to make the motorcycle do the work. This, too, is great fun, because it requires attention, split-second decision making, perfect hand-eye coordination, good timing, and seamless motorcycle inputs to do it right and squirt out of the way of a disaster.

That sort of thing doesn't come easily, but it makes for a heck of a good time practicing, learning, making discoveries, overcoming obstacles, and working up to that level of skill.

If you've done your homework and developed good riding strategies and skills, you've got most of your problems covered. But when something slips past your first two lines of defense (and eventually, something will), all you have left is what you're wearing. Get the best riding gear you can afford, relish all the funny looks, and have fun with the silly questions you'll get from the

Overconfidence: The sneakiest kind of inexperience.

mouth-breathers: When they ask, "Isn't it a little hot for that stuff?" just say, "Yeah, but it's a dry heat." When they ask sarcastically, "Cold out?" say, "It was when I left (insert someplace about 500 miles away and much, much colder) this morning." When they're trying to be nice and they say, "You look hot," say, "Thanks, you're not so bad yourself." Like I said, motorcycles are conversation-starters.

What People Say and What People Mean Number 1: "You're Crazy"

When your nonriding friends, family, and loved ones learn that you've decided to ride a motorcycle, it's not uncommon to get strange looks, shaking heads, and the mumbled words, "You're crazy if you want to ride one of them murder-cycles."

Some of these people will make jokes about filling out your donor card and making sure your life insurance is up to date; others will actively try to talk you out of it. You'll hear all sorts of horror stories. "Uncle Cleatus had a bike once. . . . " "My old roommate went for a ride with a friend back in college . . . and he rode the Harley about eight feet up the telephone pole guy wire." All these stories end badly, usually with the dismemberment or severe bruising of someone who otherwise had a lot going for them, or would have gone on to become president or a successful plumber.

While these people mean well, all they're really saying is that they're not willing to take on the added risks of riding a motorcycle. They've learned everything they need to learn, and "those bikes are just plain dangerous."

Basically, they're just telling you that you are braver than they are. That's as it should be. Motorcycling is not for everyone. Riders are not necessarily risk takers; they're just willing to accept more risk in return for the rewards of riding. You can calmly explain to them that motorcycles are just machines. They do only what the rider tells them to do . . . and failing to respect a motorcycle's capabilities can land a rider into a world of hurt. And sure, riders are more vulnerable in traffic, but a thoughtful, trained, and skilled rider can negotiate traffic and hazards just as well as everyone else, and have more fun doing it.

Concerned friends or family members trying to talk you out of riding a motorcycle are probably picturing something like this, or remembering way back when it was them taking the risks. Your best defense is to show them that you're taking it seriously, wearing your gear, and doing your best to be smart about it.

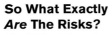

So What Exactly *Are* The Risks?

The Rider. More than anything else, it is the rider who poses the biggest risk to him or herself. Mental mistakes like dumb positioning in traffic, assuming another motorist is paying attention to *you* and not his double-bacon greaseburger, or heading off into traffic half asleep, angry, or drunk can place you in a bad situation—one that you may not be able to escape. A lack of training and skill at the controls can make even something simple like avoiding a pothole filled with rusty nails and poisonous spiders at fifteen miles per hour impossible. Inexperience and overconfidence (the sneakiest form of inexperience) can mean that one otherwise manageable hazard can put you into Motorcyclist Information Overload (MIO). You'll freeze up and crash because you simply couldn't sort it all out in time. A rider's head, body, and attitude all have to be in the game. We'll look a little closer at MIO in Chapter 5.

The Other Guy. You have to share the road with about 150 million other people. According to late twentieth century folklore, most of these people consider themselves "better than average" drivers. This means that most of them *think* they're better drivers than they actually are. Yikes.

We know that nobody's out there deliberately trying to run motorcyclists down, but the fact is, most nonriders simply don't know much about motorcycles and don't pay much attention. Bikes are smaller, and it's harder for motorists to judge their speed and distance. It's also easier to intrude on a rider's space without realizing it. And let's face it, most drivers are human (except for those obviously from another planet) and they make mistakes. When you're in a car and someone makes a mistake, you have a steel cage to protect you. On your bike, when someone makes a mistake—no matter if it's you or them—it can cost you your fingers. Or your head.

The Environment. Different types of roads have different types of hazards. The traffic you have to deal with and the risks you face on an interstate freeway are different from the ones you face in the inner city's

You have to share the road with about 150 million other people. According to late twentieth century folklore, most of these people consider themselves "better than average" drivers. This means that most of them think *they're better drivers than they actually are. Yikes.*

hustle and bustle. Rush hours, heavy traffic, high speeds, green lights changing to yellow, merging lanes, and solid immovable objects like buildings and parked cars all throw freaky curve balls at you. The surface of the road also makes a huge difference in the risks you face. A patch of sand, radiator fluid, or diesel fuel in the wrong place at the wrong time can put you upside down in the ditch before you can say, "What's that smell?" And wind, rain, blinding sun, and late-night darkness can worm their way into your otherwise safe ride and cause problems both for you and everybody else.

Motorcyclists are a different breed. They think, act, and dress differently from everyone else. They're willing to accept the

*Motorcyclists are
a different breed.
They think, act,
and dress differently
from everyone else.*

It may surprise you to learn that the biggest risk to motorcycle riders… is motorcycle riders. Only about half of all motorcycle crashes involve another driver, and in those crashes the rider almost always shares the blame. When assessing your risks, look first to yourself.

risks that go along with motorcycling because the rewards, like challenge, adventure, and fun, are so great. Smart riders think hard about what they're doing. They're constantly working to minimize their risks, improve, grow as riders, and

Diesel Fuel: Never thought about it before, huh? Trucks spill diesel fuel all the time. It leaves a puddle. The puddle is like ice. Think about it.

wring a little more out of everyday life than most people. Welcome to the club.

Recommended Reading:
Motorcycle magazines. Start getting a feel for styles of bikes, terminology, and the subjects that interest motorcyclists.

GETTING STARTED

NCE YOU'VE COME TO UNDERSTAND HOW MOTORCYCLE RIDERS ARE UNLIKE ANYONE ELSE ON THE PLANET, YOU'RE READY FOR STEP ONE: SELECTING A BIKE.

Picking out your new ride is terrific fun, poring nose-first through magazines, loitering around dealerships, ogling other people's bikes, searching the Internet. But it will quickly become obvious that about a million different bikes are out there, and every one of them is a little different, and every rider has a unique reason for owning the one he or she owns.

This will be your first exposure to Motorcyclist Information Overload. The number of choices is overwhelming and can easily leave you paralyzed with indecision. (An easy solution, and one adopted by more motorcyclists than I can name, is to skip the whole this-one-or-that-one process and just buy every bike that strikes your fancy. Welcome to garage-space *hell*.)

So which one should you get? As a beginner, your choices will be narrowed down quite a bit, which helps, but there's still a nearly unlimited number from which to choose. So you'll need to ask yourself some key questions and select some important equipment *first*, then find the bike that's right for you and start the process of breaking the ice with your new friend.

While it may seem like a lot to take in all at once, by asking yourself some hard questions and knowing your limitations, you can whittle down the choices and pick a bike that's perfect for you. If you're like many motorcyclists, you'll own that bike forever, and instead of trading it for something else, you'll simply add

Dealer or private seller? Some riders hate using dealers, but look at it philosophically: If you didn't let them sell you the parts and service and stuff you need at a markup, they wouldn't be there to provide you the parts and service and stuff you need when you truly need it. You might save some money buying a bike from a private party, but is it worth it when you have to drive 50 miles to buy an oil filter because your local dealership tanked?

Self-Evaluation

How do you plan to use your motorcycle? We asked a similar question in Chapter 1, but now let's get even more specific. Do you want it one day a week, or several? Do you plan to ride on the freeway, or with passengers? Do you hope to take long trips to faraway places, or will you just use it to explore the nearby on the weekends? Will you use it every day for commuting? Will you take it off-road to remote scenic overlooks, or will it stay on the pavement every moment of its life? Are you hoping to save money on gas, insurance, or parking? Do you want people to notice you or leave you alone?

Having a definite goal for what you want to accomplish as a motorcyclist will give you a good place to start when picking out your first bike. Your goals will probably change along the way, and you'll decide you want a different bike in a year or two. For now, however, make a decision and stick to it. There are simply too many choices out there to leave it open-ended.

Gear Up!

Smart riders will tell you to buy your riding gear first. And that's good advice. It's way too easy to overstep your finances when buying a bike and have absolutely no money left for good protective gear. You'll be a sitting duck (with no feathers!) on a great bike. Instead, buy the helmet, boots, gloves, pants, and jacket first and use what's left over to go bike shopping. Then you'll be a well-dressed motorcyclist on a bike you can afford. It's a lot easier to convince concerned loved ones that you're doing it the right way when you can say, "At least I bought the protective gear *first*."

Plan on spending at least $450, or as much as $2,100, for your first set of riding gear. If you don't have enough money to buy gear *and* a bike, then hold off on getting into motorcycling until you do.

> *Smart riders will tell you to buy your riding gear first. Then you'll be a well-dressed motorcyclist on a bike you can afford.*

Power Ranger—or Smart Rider? While protection from injury is the ultimate goal, good riding gear will also make you more comfortable and more visible to other drivers. When you're comfortable, you're more alert and better able to detect hazards and manage traffic to avoid problems. High visibility—making it easier for others to see you—will help you avoid crashes in the first place. If you're overly concerned about standing out from the crowd, you're missing the point. Buy the best gear you can afford, and buy gear that you love, so that you'll love wearing it.

Since motorcyclists can least afford to be distracted on the road, the smartest riders wear clothing that insulates them from the elements.

Comfort First, Visibility Next, Protection Last

The most important reason to wear riding gear is for comfort. Visibility comes second. Even though it may seem like protection in a crash is the true purpose and priority of riding gear, it's way down at third on the list. Your goal is to use protective gear to prevent crashes in the first place, and only rely on its protective qualities if you absolutely have to.

Comfort. All the crap you've never had to deal with in a car—temperature

You're not just trying to stand out like a sore thumb; you're trying to stand out like a sore thumb on a pink elephant riding a pogo stick. Don't fall into the trap of trying to look like a "traditional biker" with black leather or camouflage clothing. You're in the twenty-first century now. There are better ways to protect yourself.

variations, sun, wind, rain, heat, cold, bugs, blowing dust, flying debris, and sand—you get a front-row seat for on your motorcycle. If you don't guard against them, they go to work on your concentration immediately. The heat and vibration of the motorcycle itself can be intrusive, as well. Since motorcyclists can least afford to be distracted on the road, the smartest riders wear clothing that insulates them from the elements. Controlling the effects of the environment, especially the extreme effects of heat, wind, and cold (heat exhaustion, dehydration, and hypothermia) can help you stay comfortable, which means fewer distractions, better concentration, and less fatigue, both mental and physical.

Visibility. Even though a rider, in theory, has complete control over everything that happens on the road, it's still wise to make yourself as conspicuous as possible. You want to give other drivers every possible opportunity to notice you and give you the space you need to ride. A brightly colored jacket and helmet helps draw attention to your presence on the road. Not only that, but a colorful display (think peacock or circus clown) of expensive motorcycle gear also shows the world that you're very attuned to your own safety, which may have positive side effects as well.

Protection. Good gear can reduce or prevent injuries in a crash. Plastic composites, leather, and modern textiles (like nylon) with padding and armor can take some or all of the bite out of a mistake on the road. When you fall off your bike, you're going to hit *something*, even if it's just the ground. Adding a sacrificial layer or two of "skin" will lower your chances of suffering through a dramatic lifestyle change when all you did was over-look a puddle of antifreeze at a stoplight.

A Note about Conformity

It's really tempting to buy the same riding gear that everybody else wears, especially the do-rags, sunglasses, leather vests, and chaps. (Peer pressure is alive and well in the motorcycle community.) But those

people aren't responsible for the skin on your butt or the roundness of your skull. You are. Buy what makes the most sense to you, based on information you trust, and *not* what you think everyone else will accept or what you think looks cool. Gear serves a very important purpose—and that purpose is *not* fashion—and motorcyclists will surprise you with their open-mindedness. While they might give you some good-natured ribbing about your "snowmobile suit" or "brain bucket," they will respect your right to choose what you wear and when you wear it.

Do-rag: That bandana-looking thing that many riders wear on their head to look like a pirate.

You don't have to look like this to be a motorcycle rider. And while imitation is said to be the sincerest form of flattery, it may not save your bacon when your front tire washes out in a sandy corner and you end up sliding face-first across the road wearing only a T-shirt and sunglasses. Mark Langello

Gear serves a very important purpose—and that purpose is not fashion—and motorcyclists will surprise you with their open-mindedness.

If you had to tumble from a moving vehicle, how would you dress for the jump? Would your clothing reflect the weather that day, or the worst-case scenario? There's merit to the saying, "Dress for the slide, not the ride."

How do you feel about your pretty face? Want anything for that?

Making the Leap

As a new rider, you're prone to making a few simple mistakes as you learn to ride. Even the little blunders can have a big impact on your future as a rider, so let's look at protective gear from a real-world perspective. Picture yourself wearing street clothes on a hot summer day: shorts, sandals, and a T-shirt. Now imagine yourself in the back of a pickup truck with the tailgate down. You're lying on the tailgate, your body parallel to the road. You're probably three or four feet in the air and the ground beneath you is made of asphalt. The asphalt's plenty warm in the summer sunshine.

Now you're going to close your eyes and imagine rolling out of the back of the truck onto the ground. If the truck's not moving, it's probably not a *huge* deal—you can use your hands, back, shoulders, butt, or whatever to cushion the fall. But even at 0 miles per hour, you could still land awkwardly, maybe banging your elbow or knee or scraping some skin. Either way, you wouldn't want

to just roll out of the truck. You'd probably rather stand up and jump out so you can land on your feet. Riders on motorcycles are rarely given the choice whether to roll or land on their feet. When the bike tumbles, the rider usually tumbles too. So picture yourself rolling out of the truck onto the ground.

Now, what if you had to do this with the truck moving at 5 miles per hour? At this point, you'd opt for some more clothing: blue jeans, a denim shirt, some high-top shoes, and maybe some knee and elbow pads, just to be on the safe side. How do you feel about your pretty face? Want anything for that?

Now think about trying this stunt at 15 miles per hour. The shoes are probably still sufficient, but now street clothes might not stay put. You don't want your shirt riding up and letting your bare back or belly hit the pavement. Might be time to consider getting something that's made for tumbling on pavement, like leather. You're probably thinking about a pair of gloves, too, and definitely knee and elbow

Even at a modest 30 miles per hour this is still likely to hurt, even with the gear. Imagine how bad it'd hurt if you were wearing your swimsuit.

And so it goes. The higher the speed, the longer you'll tumble, or the harder you'll hit whatever it is you're tumbling toward.

pads. (I fell on my hands and knees a lot when I was a kid. I seem to remember it hurt like hell.) Protecting your head with your hands might be difficult—time to don a little headgear, do you think?

How do you feel about 30 miles per hour? That's pretty fast. At this point you definitely want a second skin. A throwaway layer. Covering your arms, legs, torso, feet, and hands. Good leather, too. Thick leather. Not that lightweight crap they sell at clothing stores. You want motorcycle-specific clothing, something that'll last for several seconds of crashing.

At 30 miles per hour, you're probably second-guessing your desire to leave the relative safety of the moving vehicle. Your brain is backpedaling. Maybe you can get the driver to slow down to about 5 miles per hour again? Is there a good reason to be doing this? Keep imagining:

Wind that truck up to 60 miles per hour. Feel the wind in your hair? Nice, isn't it? It's only nice if you get to stay in the truck—or on your bike. The world doesn't work like that, though—nobody

chooses the worst case. If you fall off, you're sure to get hurt without a good layer of gear. Now you want the works: full coverage, durable material, padding at the shoulders, elbows, forearms, hips, and knees—all the pointy places. You'll also want something to protect your spine and your head. I want sturdy boots and thick sturdy gloves. (You're searching desperately for some soft-looking asphalt.)

And so it goes. The higher the speed, the longer you'll tumble, or the harder you'll hit whatever it is you're tumbling toward. To survive a fall from a bike at any speed without injury, you need a second skin. Even at 5 miles per hour you can change your good looks forever. There's a reason motorcycle racers can often walk away from 100-mile-per-hour crashes more embarrassed than hurt: They care as much about the gear they wear as they do the bike they ride. If you want to walk the motorcyclist walk, and talk the motorcyclist talk, you're going to want to wear the motorcyclist gear.

If you buy nothing else in the way of protective gear, buy a good pair of safety glasses. Your eyes provide you with 99 percent of everything you need to know on a bike—don't leave them hanging in the wind.

Wile E. Coyote jokes aside, goggles make a good alternative to safety glasses, but are more difficult to fit under a helmet and not always well-ventilated.

Your eyes provide you with 99 percent of everything you need to know on a bike—don't leave them hanging in the wind.

Watch out! There are "novelty" helmets (plastic G.I. Joe salad bowls with chinstraps) for revolutionaries who refuse to conform to a helmet law. Look for the DOT or Snell sticker already stuck on the helmet if you live in a state with a helmet law. (The fake helmets' DOT stickers are sold separately "on the side," like a house salad with dressing on the side for those fussy Sally Albright types.)

To choose a style, you'll need to decide what exactly you want to accomplish with your helmet. Do you want to protect your brain (half helmet), your brain and skull, (three-quarter helmet), or your brain, skull, and face (full-faced helmet)? The most coverage possible, a full-faced helmet should fit snugly and should not move around on your head. Your skin and scalp should move with it. Be careful of the face shield: It's easily scratched. Use warm water, mild soap and a soft cloth or sponge. Never use wood products like napkins, tissues, or paper towels, which will wreck it in a hurry.

Some riders will swear that Helmet Brand X is "safer" than Helmet Brand Y, but it's far more important to choose based on comfort. Every manufacturer has a slightly different idea of what a head is shaped like, and every rider's head is a little different, so you'll need to try on a few different brands and sizes to find the one that fits you best. Courtesy American Honda

A helmet will take a little getting used to, and may even be distracting at first, but learning to wear it will be worth the effort. You'll need one for your training class anyway, so get a good one to start with and give it at least a few weeks of use before you decide whether you like it or not. Courtesy Kawasaki

Head First

Eye Protection: $10–$200. Almost all the information a rider uses on a motorcycle is visual, so your absolute first priority is to protect your eyes. On a motorcycle you're constantly bombarded with ultraviolet light, wind, rain, insects, and blowing sand and dirt that can cause enormous strain on your eyes or even blind you to the outside world. Before you buy anything else, get a decent pair of shatter-resistant glasses with clear lenses. Shielding your eyes will allow you to ride safer and for longer periods without getting all droopy.

Helmet: $60–$500. Generally, all helmets work the same way and perform similarly in crashes. Helmets certified by DOT and/or Snell have passed tests to ensure they offer a standard of crash protection. What you pay for are added features like fit, finish, graphics, comfort, padding, venting systems, visor quality, and other

neat features like breath guards, sun visors, aerodynamics, etc. Get one that you feel comfortable with, in fit and appearance, so you'll enjoy wearing it.

A helmet should fit comfortably and snugly when you first try it on, especially around the cheeks and eyes. It should make you feel just a little bit claustrophobic. If there are any pressure points, especially around your forehead, ears, or temples, try the next larger size. A lid that is even a little loose at the store will be floppy and miserable (and useless) within a few months. Helmets loosen up within a few weeks, so if you're between sizes at the dealership, go with the smaller one.

A helmet is not the magic bullet that everyone seems to think it is! There are no guarantees. A recent study found that brightly colored helmets make riders more visible to other drivers, but remember, it's just a piece of equipment, basically a hard plastic shell lined with expanded polystyrene (i.e., picnic cooler foam).

A helmet should fit comfortably and snugly when you first try it on, especially around the cheeks and eyes.

On the Down Low

Boots: $100–$300. Once you've got your eye and head protection figured out, it's time to go look at some boots. Motorcycle boots are next on the list because foot and ankle injuries are common in motorcycle crashes (many times caused by the motorcycle itself). They also can keep your feet dry, give you a good grip on the ground at stops, and make it easier to use the footpegs and controls to brake and shift—not to mention giving you good insulation against innocuous hazards like bouncing road stones, low-flying birds, scurrying animals, and slow-moving amphibious turtlemonsters.

The best boots are leather, waterproof, and provide solid coverage for your feet, ankles, and lower legs. More subtle styles can double as street shoes, or you can go for the full-on protection of competition racing boots with armor, toe sliders, and plates to protect your soft parts.

The best boots are leather, waterproof, and provide solid coverage for your feet, ankles, and lower legs.

(Top) They don't have to be expensive or heavy-duty to protect well. All-purpose boots look nice, keep your feet dry, and fit well enough under your pant legs to pass as regular shoes. Note the low heel—important for working the foot controls while keeping your feet on the pegs. Courtesy Alpinestars

(Bottom) It may be tempting to buy a cheaper pair of street shoes that look like motorcycle boots, but don't do it—as in all riding gear, you want items that are designed for riding a motorcycle. Fashionable boots might complete your image, but they don't tend to hold up as well when the chips are down and you're sliding down the road underneath your bike.

(Top) *When trying on gloves, it's not enough to know that they fit okay. You need to simulate gripping the handlebars so you can get a good feel for the way they'll fit when you're actually riding. These deerskin gloves offer great protection, great feel and sensitivity, and can be washed with soap and water that might otherwise ruin normal leather.*

(Bottom) *If you want to ride like a pro, it's not a bad idea to dress like one. Spend the dough and get good gloves meant for motorcycling. Riding for any period of time without decent gloves can make your hands tired, sore, and numb. And when falling down, at any speed, people instinctively put their hands out. When the road is rushing beneath bare skin and fingers at 30-60 miles per hour, you can turn your body's most important tools into painful, bloody stumps in a matter of seconds.*

Good gloves generally come precurved and the seams are ironed down to better conform to the shape of the handlebars and provide better comfort when closed around the handgrips for long periods of time.

Hands and Control

Gloves: $30–$100. A close second to motorcycle helmets in making riding more enjoyable, the gloves you wear can make a huge difference in how well you ride and how much fun it is. Gloves are absolutely necessary for protecting your hands from sun, wind, rain, and flying objects. They also mute the vibrations from the bike and offer a little squishy padding to help work the controls.

That said, the only way to go is with leather, deerskin, or elkskin gloves made specifically for motorcycling. Motorcycle gloves use thicker and stronger hides and stitching for better protection and good control of the bike's levers and switches. Good gloves generally come precurved and the seams are ironed down to better conform to the shape of the handlebars and provide better comfort when closed around the handgrips for long periods of time. Some gloves come with armor on the back side and knuckles, and extra padding on the palm and heel for better protection.

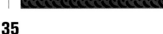

Good gear should have some bright colors (red, blue, yellow, white) with nighttime-reflective material on it, in order to help other drivers see you. If you live in a state that has wide temperature ranges, look carefully for gear that has zip-in liners, perforation, or other cold/warm accoutrements that will affect your comfort at the temperature extremes.

When trying on gear, make sure you "test it out" by assuming a riding position, seated, legs apart, knees bent, with your arms stretched out in front of you.

The Body

Jacket and pants: $250–$1,000. Okay, you've got your extremities figured out; it's time to get to the fun stuff. Your riding jacket and pants help you stand out in traffic and insulate you from the effects of weather and wind. Like everything else, it's important to pick out gear that you like so you'll enjoy wearing it. But it can also be expensive—there's a lot of square footage to cover—so pretend you're out shopping on your birthday. In fact, consider the jacket/pants combo you pick out to be your birthday suit.

When it comes to the most obvious of riding gear, choices are nearly limitless. Some work well, some work too well, and some don't work well at all. Generally, you get what you pay for.

It makes good sense to spend some time shopping different vendors, asking around, and finding out what you get when you lay down your money—as well as how well it holds up.

When trying on gear, make sure you "test it out" by assuming a riding position, seated, legs apart, knees bent, with your arms stretched out in front of you. Your pants should not bind or constrict you or pull up to your knees when you sit down, and your jacket should not ride up your back when you reach out for the handlebars. The legs and sleeves should be extra long to accommodate riding. The closures at the waist, ankles, wrists, and neck should be adjustable to keep the garment in place and the wind out.

Don't waste your money on anything that doesn't have at least some body armor sewn in to protect your pointy parts: elbows, shoulders, and knees. You can usually find gear that also has armor or padding on the chest, back, and hips. A little bit of extra armor goes a long way when you start a-tumbling. The best armor is hard plastic backed by impact-absorbing foam.

The stereotypical leather motorcycle jacket gives you comfort and protection, but lacks visibility, and good visibility can help prevent trouble. If you absolutely have to go with the outlaw biker look, strongly consider a reflective safety vest (worn over the jacket) and a brightly colored helmet.

The biggest decision you need to make is whether to go with textile (synthetic) gear or with leather. Leather is ultimately the best way to go, but in the real world, motorcyclists have to compromise. Most riders agree that leather is the best for crash protection, but modern synthetic jackets and pants come very close in that department. Leather can be crashed multiple times without needing repair, but textiles usually need to be repaired after a crash.

Leather can be crashed multiple times without needing repair, but textiles usually need to be repaired after a crash.

However, what makes textiles so appealing is that they don't get ruined when they get wet, they can be thrown in the washing machine, and they're usually cheaper than leather. They're also more versatile: Good synthetic clothing is adaptable to different temperatures, while leather is not. Many of the synthetic products are waterproof and breathable with removable liners.

Selecting a Bike

By now you're chomping at the bit to go pick out a motorcycle. Okay. You've waited long enough. You've gone about it the right way, by asking yourself the right questions, priming yourself for the task ahead, and taking the time to pick out good riding gear. You have a pretty good idea what you want. Okay, let's go.

The most important thing at this point is to find a bike that's the right size for you, physically. Buy a bike too big for you and you look like a little kid riding an oversized Big Wheel. Buy a bike too small and you look like a gorilla riding a toaster. You should be able to plant your feet flat on the ground while sitting on the bike, and you should be able to pick it up if it falls over. "Bike size" is closely related to engine size, so you can narrow your selection criteria down to a few tantalizing choices based solely on displacement (normally measured in cubic centimeters, or "cc"). Ideally, set a limit of 500 cc for a four-cylinder engine or 700 cc for a two-cylinder engine. Anything greater than that can get unwieldy and make it difficult for you to learn.

You're going to pick out your first bike based on the type of bikes that appeal to you and the way you plan to ride. For every "ideal" or dream bike, there are a few smaller, more manageable bikes that will get you started in that direction. You should deliberately plan to buy something to cut your teeth on, with the intention of riding it for a year or two and then buying your dream bike after you've got a few miles and mishaps under your belt.

Very rarely is a person's first bike the only one they ever own, so don't worry about making a commitment to a bike that doesn't make your heart pitter-patter. It's not like the dating game. You don't have to worry about hurting a motorcycle's feelings. You can buy a bike specifically for the purpose of using it, get your feet wet, then without guilt cast it aside and take up with one that really turns your crank.

You're going to pick out your first bike based on the type of bikes that appeal to you and the way you plan to ride.

The most important thing at this point is to find a bike that's the right size for you, physically.

Short riders and women will generally find that cruisers between 125 and 650 cc or small standard bikes between 250 and 550 cc work best for learning; bigger or taller riders will be better off on larger standards between 450 and 700 cc or dual-sport motorcycles from 250 to 650 cc. Modern 600 cc sportbikes are not good beginner bikes: They're too high-strung, expensive, and powerful.

The Standard All-Purpose Two-Wheeler

The real virtue of a standard is that it can do practically anything you ask of it. You can tour, commute, sport ride, run errands, cruise the boulevard, go off-road, carry passengers, etc., nearly as well as you can on bikes designed for those purposes. While a standard may not be the best at any *one* of those things, it can pull a close second-best in *all* those things, making it a versatile, practical machine that's well worth the money.

Beginner Standards to Consider
Honda Nighthawk 250, 450; CB125, 400, 450
Kawasaki W650
Suzuki GN 125; Suzuki GS 400, GS 425, GS 450, GS 500, GS 550; SV 650
Yamaha XS 400, XS 650; Maxim XJ 550

Another way to look at standards is to consider dual-sport bikes similar to the BMW F650—all-purpose standards, and then some. Dual-sports tend to have peppy, indestructible, easy-to-use engines, superior suspensions (which in some cases lead to too-tall seat heights), and an upright seating position that allows you to see over and ahead of traffic. For these reasons they make excellent street bikes, even though "dual-sport" refers to their ability to be ridden on- or off-road.

Dual-Sports to Consider
Aprilia Pegaso 650
BMW F650
Honda FT500; XL 600, XL 650; NX 650; XR 650
Kawasaki KE 100; KL 250; KLR 250, 650; KLX 450
Suzuki DR 200, DR 350, DR-Z400, DR 650
Yamaha TW 200; XT 225, XT 350, XT 550, XT 600

The real virtue of a standard is that it can do practically anything you ask of it.

Standards make great first bikes, no matter what type of riding you hope to do. If you're planning on using your bike solely for commuter duty, envision long trips touring the countryside—or if you don't yet know exactly how you will want to use your bike—you'd best go with a standard for a first bike. They generally get good gas mileage, are low cost and low maintenance, are cheap to insure, and don't distract you with bells and whistles so you can take the time to learn what you really want in a motorcycle. Courtesy Kawasaki

The nearly irresistible CB Nighthawk: User-friendly, tall enough for bigger riders, bulletproof in engine and design, and rather sporty. Courtesy American Honda

Harley-Davidson's entry level motorcycle, the Buell Blast (500) is lightweight with a low seat height, great fun to ride, sporty, and feels somehow smaller than other bikes half its size. Courtesy Buell Motorcycles USA

Dual-sports tend to have peppy, indestructible, easy-to-use engines, superior suspensions, and an upright seating position that allows you to see over and ahead of traffic.

Unusual looking, tall, technologically advanced, freakyfun, the BMW singles are a hoot and great learner bikes. Courtesy BMW

The comfy easy-chair seating and foot position on a cruiser make it a perfect way to escape the noise and pressure of everyday life while not getting too far from home. This bike is meant for strolling along, enjoying the weather, and feeling your troubles slipping away beneath you. Courtesy Kawasaki

If your motorcycling goal is to have a traditional, good-looking, and mean-sounding bike, a cruiser-style bike is what you want.

The Virago comes in a million sizes. The smaller bikes are bulletproof, have a low seat height, sport a V-Twin engine, are pretty sharp looking and fun to ride. Courtesy Yamaha Motor Corp.

The Cruiser: Style and Function

If your motorcycling goal is to have a traditional, good-looking, and mean-sounding bike to use for transportation and/or leisurely rides, a cruiser-style bike is what you want. Cruisers usually offer a low seat height good for smaller or shorter riders, a low center of gravity for good stability, and comfortable seating and riding positions. They tend toward the longer and heavier end of the motor-cycling spectrum, and sometimes that can work against you when you're learning. On the other hand, because they're a little bulkier, the engine and power is usually a little more manageable, and you're less likely to have your bike jackrabbit out from under you when you accidentally pop the clutch at a stop sign.

Beginner Cruisers to Consider
Honda Rebel 250, 450; Magna 500,
    Shadow 500, 600, 700
Kawasaki Eliminator 125; Vulcan LTD 500
Suzuki GZ 250; Savage 650
Yamaha XS 250; Virago 250, 535,
    V-Star 650

Honda's Shadow is a really great way to cut your teeth. It's got a beautiful design, low seat height, good power, and a big fat rear tire that will impress even your nonriding friends. Courtesy American Honda.

One of the more popular cruisers for beginners and experienced riders alike, the V-Star is breathtaking to look at, maneuverable, reliable, and has a seat height low enough to accommodate smaller riders. Courtesy Yamaha Motor Corp.

The bike you're lusting after is almost not the right bike to learn on.

What People Say and What People Mean
Number 2: "Start Small"

If you're going approach motorcycling from a holistic perspective, your first real act of intelligence will be what you choose for your first bike.

When experienced riders tell you to start small, they don't exactly mean that you should start on a little bike (though as a rule of thumb, it's not bad advice). What they mean is that you should start on a bike that you'll be able to handle physically, financially, and psychologically. The bike you're lusting after is almost always not the right bike to learn on.

This means starting on a bike of a size and power level that won't immediately overwhelm you while you're still learning to keep it balanced and work the controls. It's hard enough to get basic motorcycle handling mastered without trying to rein in a bike that wants to continually leap from your grasp or crush you in your garage when you forget to put the sidestand down. Buying an older used bike means when you tip it over or crash it (and you will), the repair bills won't cost you more than your first car did. Most importantly, starting small means your focus is still on you—your priority is not what bike you own, but learning how to ride. A state-of-the-art machine will whisper to you to do things you're not ready to do yet. A big, expensive bike will make you look and feel like a better rider than you are, and you absolutely do not need that sort of distraction this early in the ballgame.

Too many riders make the mistake of buying the bike they're in love with for their first bike. These bikes will typically answer the question, "What is the best bike?" when what a beginner really wants to know is, "What is the best bike for me?" It is only with heroic self-restraint that most new riders can commit to buying a bike they know they'll outgrow in a year or two. But the riders who do are rewarded with a quicker learning curve and low cost, which leaves lots of room to practice, experiment, and have fun.

Even the meekest of these bikes is way more than what is useful on the street, but if you want the best bike for corner carving or racing, the sportbike is the only way to go.

The quintessential, full-on, race-replica sportbike. Trick suspension, ultra-high-performance engine, aggressive riding position, and helter-skelter graphics make these bikes stand out in every way. Even the meekest of these bikes is way more than what is useful on the street, but if you want the best bike for corner carving or racing, the sportbike is the only way to go. These bikes are not suitable for beginners.

The 250 Interceptors are smooth, deceptively quick and sporty, handle great, and they're reasonably cheap. The 500 sports a V-four engine with an unforgettable sound. Courtesy American Honda.

The Sportbike:
Vivid Technology

Riders who want to draw attention to themselves visually and plan to put their motorcycle through its paces like a sports car should be thinking about sportbikes.

Beginning Sportbikes to Consider
Aprilia RS 50
Buell Blast 500
Ducati Monster 600, 620
Honda Interceptor 250, 500; Hawk 650
Kawasaki Ninja 250, 500; EX 500; KZ 550
Suzuki GS 500, SV650

Suzuki's GS 500: The little motorcycle that could. It's versatile, reliable, lightweight, and comfortable. Best yet, when you get bored of it you can strip it down and turn it into a way-bad race bike. Courtesy American Suzuki

The little Ninjas offer unparalleled performance, great handling, and the good looks of a sportbike. Courtesy Kawasaki

45

The Ideal Beginner Bike

The ideal beginner bike has to be a compromise between large and small, powerful and wimpy, good-looking, and utilitarian. What you're looking for is a medium-sized standard with a small-displacement, two-cylinder engine, good brakes, suspension, and reliability, sporty looks, good mileage, lots of room for accessories and modification, a modest price tag, and reasonable insurance.

The SV650 technically fits into the standard category and can be modified to fit nearly any rider's physique and riding style. Less stable than a cruiser, its higher center of gravity and quirkier handling teach you smoothness that transfers nicely to the big whopper you have your heart set on. More stable and less powerful than a sportbike, it still offers sporty handling and allows you to get a feel for aggressive sport riding without the twitchiness and raw power that goes along with sportbikes. The SV650 is also a popular bike with readily available parts, accessories, and plenty of used models on the market at reasonable prices. If you don't want to shop around and just want to get a bike and ride, the SV650 is the way to go.

What you're looking for is a medium-sized standard with a small-displacement, two-cylinder engine, good brakes, suspension, and reliability, sporty looks, good mileage, lots of room for accessories and modification, a modest price tag, and reasonable insurance.

In this author's opinion, Suzuki can claim to offer the best all-around beginner bike in the SV650. Light, nimble, quick, adaptable, fun, and cheap, it's easy to ride—which means you'll learn very quickly—yet versatile enough to keep you entertained for a while. If and when you finally outgrow it, there'll be other beginners waiting in line to take the reins. Courtesy American Suzuki

An "Ambassador" for Motorcycling

Once you've pulled the trigger and bought all your riding gear and your first bike, you officially become a representative of motorcyclists everywhere. Take your new image seriously. Hollywood and the media portray motorcycle riders as drug-snorting outlaw gang members, reckless adrenaline-junkie stunt riders, and antisocial hooligans who are a menace to society. It's up to you to show the world that you're not, and that they can't always believe what they see on TV.

Avoid looking and behaving in such a way as to perpetuate negative stereotypes, and work hard to demonstrate to others that you're no different from anyone else. Your family and friends already know that, so start with them. You're not rebelling against society or in the grips of a midlife crisis (well, maybe you are, that's still okay), you just happen to prefer a more windblown, nimble, and sexy form of transportation than they do. When they realize that, they may realize that all those other scary motorcyclists are ordinary people, too. Score one for the good guys.

Recommended Reading:

The Complete Idiot's Guide to Motorcycles by Darwin Holmstrom: This book is a good resource for comparing and selecting gear and a bike, as well as lots of other valuable information about motorcycles and riding.

The Motorcycle Book by Alan Seeley: General information about bikes, gear, training, and licensing, but good detail on motorcycle mechanics and what to look for when buying a used bike.

www.totalmotorcycle.com and **www.webBikeWorld.com**: These are great online comparisons of motorcycles geared toward new riders looking to get into motorcycling and buying their first bikes.

Avoid looking and behaving in such a way as to perpetuate negative stereotypes, and work hard to demonstrate to others that you're no different from anyone else.

Big Secret Number 2: The Centerstand

An oft-overlooked necessity on a beginner bike is the much-maligned centerstand. Similar to a kickstand, but oh so much more, a centerstand lifts the bike off the ground with a flip of the lever, making maintenance a whole heck of a lot easier. Parking the bike on the centerstand helps ensure that it will not get tipped over, and you can do things like practice your riding posture and riding techniques while stationary in the garage. It's particularly cool for when little kids come over and want to check out your new bike. Climb on it all they want, it's almost impossible for them to tip it over.

There's a lot of mystery surrounding how to use the centerstand, but it's not that difficult. Park the bike on its sidestand with the front tire pointed straight ahead. (It's a little easier to do this with the bike pointed slightly uphill.) Allow a little room for the bike to rock backward when you lift it. Lift the bike from the left side. Have a friend steady the bike from the other side the first couple of times you try this.

Place your boot on the centerstand's foot lever and press down until the centerstand just touches the ground. Hold on to the left handgrip with your left hand, and with your right, find a solid part of the bike to lift with—the frame, passenger handhold, even the footpeg mount—ideally a few inches below your beltline. Tilt the bike away from you until it's straight up and down and both sides of the centerstand touch the ground.

To engage the centerstand, you're not so much pushing, pulling, or rocking, but "spreading" the bike top to bottom: Think of it as prying open a giant clam. As you pull upward and push downward

Similar to a kickstand, but oh so much more, a centerstand lifts the bike off the ground with a flip of the lever, making maintenance a whole heck of a lot easier.

A useful item to look for when selecting your first bike is a centerstand. Overlooking the fact that centerstands are really handy when it comes to maintenance, they are also rarely found on bikes that beginners should avoid.

simultaneously, the bike will rock backward (to your right) just a little and then drop onto the centerstand.

To get the bike off the centerstand, simply rock the bike forward. It's safest take the bike off the centerstand while you're straddling the bike. Again, have someone help you the first couple of times until you get used to it.

You have the bike ready to lift onto the centerstand: The front tire is pointed forward, your left hand on the handgrip to keep it from falling away from you, the sidestand is still down to prevent the bike from falling into you, your right hand has a firm grip and is ready to lift, and your right foot ready to press down.

To engage the centerstand, you're not so much pushing, or rocking but "spreading" the bike top to bottom: Think of it as prying open a gaint clam.

GETTING ACQUAINTED

TO A CASUAL OBSERVER, A MOTORCYCLE MAY LOOK COMPLICATED. TO A RIDER, A MOTORCYCLE LOOKS LIKE THE ONLY REASONABLE CHOICE FOR A TRIP FROM POINT A TO POINT B, A TRUSTY STEED ALWAYS RESTED AND READY TO RIDE, AND A WILLING ACCOMPLICE TO ASSIST IN WHATEVER ADVENTURES MIGHT BE JUST AROUND THE CORNER.

In its heart, a motorcycle is just a machine that will do exactly what you tell it. But there's a great deal that you need to know to keep it all in control. There's the basic fact that it must always be balanced. Your body and your mind need to do a multitude of things to maintain a margin of control and safety, and the various levers and swithches need to be used with purpose and precision.

In this chapter we'll explore how a motorcycle works, what you need to do to make it go, stop, and turn, and some basic care and maintenance tips so it's ready for fun at a moment's notice.

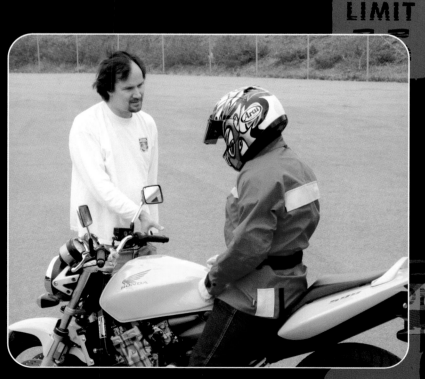

While a motorcycle's controls may seem complicated at first, they are fairly simple to use once you understand where they are, how they work, and how they work together to make the motorcycle dance.

The Point of Lowest Potential

The first and foremost thing you should know about motorcycles is that they have an innate, engineered desire to be tipped over when they're not moving, or moving very slowly. I call this "lowest potential," a mysterious force permeating the universe, and motorcyclists are especially stuck with it. Like every object, the bike is constantly seeking a place to "rest" where it will have no desire to move again.

An example of lowest potential is a boulder that has fallen off a mountaintop and come to rest in the bottom of an empty valley. Only an earthquake or a flood is going to make that boulder move. And it's not going to cause any more trouble. It's done. An example of highest potential is the same boulder teetering on the mountaintop, ready to fall onto a pile of nuclear weapons set on "hair trigger." The boulder *wants* to fall off, and the bombs *want* to explode. (Another example of high potential is the fertilized egg cell that eventually developed into Thomas Edison.)

Think about it: A motorcycle, if it's lucky, spends its life balanced on two wheels. When unattended, it's up to the sidestand or centerstand to keep it balanced. A strong wind, a brain-dead motorist backing up, or soft asphalt can give the motorcycle what it most wants—to reach its point of lowest potential, the point at which it can no longer move on its own. When you buy it, you become a lowest-potential babysitter.

This brings us back to our earlier iceberg analogy. When an ordinary motorist catches a glimpse of a motorcyclist, out riding around in the big, scary world, they might think: "Wow, that looks like a lot of fun." It *is* fun, but what they don't see is that awesome responsibility, hidden beneath the surface, of having to constantly be on guard and work against gravity just to keep the "shiny side up." Fortunately, a *moving* motorcycle has a very strong desire to *keep* moving, and it *doesn't* fall over easily. So what's the best way to keep a motorcycle from falling over? Ride it!

In its heart, a motorcycle is just a machine that will do exactly what you tell it. But there's a great deal that you need to know to keep it all in control.

(Left) When you adopt a motorcycle, you take on the responsibility to never let that thing reach its lowest potential. Your entire relationship with that bike will always have an undertone of effort, of watchfulness, of stewardship—when it's not moving or moving slowly, you're charged with keeping it from doing what it really wants to do (fall down), and instead keeping it in an "unnatural" upright state (fun and adventure balanced perfectly on two little patches of rubber).

(Above right) Here we have high potential. That tire really wants to move. All it takes is a little push. . . .

You get the whole show on the road with just your fingertips. Your left fingers make the bike go (clutch lever), your right fingers make it stop (brake lever). These are the hardest controls to master, but everything you do on a bike relies on how you squeeze these levers. You can learn to use them in a few minutes, but I promise it'll take years to perfect your technique.

Sound complicated? Never fear—you're about to learn the world's coolest juggling act.

What Does This Lever Do, and Why Would I Want to Squeeze It?

A motorcycle has six primary controls: clutch lever, front brake lever, handlebars, throttle twistgrip, shift lever, and rear brake lever. These controls make the bike go, stop, and turn. There are a good many secondary controls such as the kill switch, choke, turn signals, headlight switch, horn button, starter button, and kickstart lever. Then there are those "other" secondary controls: your eyes, ears, brain, hands, feet, thumbs, knees, elbows, shoulders, and butt. Motorcyclists use every one of these controls constantly on every ride. Sound complicated? Never fear—you're about to learn the world's coolest juggling act.

Stopping and Going

Your fingers are in charge of the clutch lever (left hand) and front brake lever (right hand), the two most important controls. The clutch makes the bike go; the front brake makes it stop.

Left Hand: Using the Clutch
The clutch controls how much of the engine's power is sent to the rear wheel. Squeezed tightly against the handgrip, 0 percent of the power will be transmitted to the wheel, equivalent to having the engine off. Released completely, 100 percent of the engine's power will go to the rear wheel. That means the bike will then do what the engine does. (Once the

---

Smart Rider Alert:

Do not attempt to operate any of the primary controls *with the engine running* **until you have read this entire chapter and completed the MSF BRC course (see Chapter 4). It's okay to do dry runs in the garage with the bike turned off, but there is absolutely nothing good that can come of doing this without quality supervision. You have been warned.**

clutch is fully released, the clutch no longer controls the bike. At that point the bike's forward motion will be turned over completely to the throttle grip.)

Expect the clutch to give you some trouble. It takes a while to get used to it; every bike's clutch has a slightly different feel. You'll stall the bike—and make the bike lurch forward suddenly—at least 500 times while you're learning. Don't get frustrated with it, just take your time, focus, and try to get a feel for it before you accidentally let it slip and send you and your bike into the nearest cornfield. And if you made the rookie mistake of buying a 600-cc or bigger sportbike for your first bike, when you head for that cornfield you'll probably be doing it on one wheel!

The first few times you use the clutch lever, ease it out *without* giving it any gas. The bike will feel lurchy and try to stall because it needs throttle, but you'll get a really good feel for exactly where the friction point (transmission of engine power) is and you'll have more control when it comes time to use both. When the bike lurches or stalls, or if it tries to leap away from you, just squeeze the clutch and try again more smoothly.

Friction Point: The point in the clutch travel at which the engine begins to engage the rear wheel and move forward.

The big secret to smooth clutch operation is to take it very, very *slowly*. As you ease the clutch lever out from the handgrip, the bike will begin to pull you forward. Hold the bike in place with your feet. Once you have the clutch lever about halfway through its friction zone, the bike will feel like a jittery horse that wants to go, Go, GO! That's what you want, but don't get excited and pop the clutch and get launched into the bushes. Hold the clutch lever right where it is, but now give it a little gas; ease it out from the grip a tiny bit more and give a little less resistance from your body; a little more throttle, ease it out a little more, and a little less body, and so on until the bike is moving and your feet are off the ground.

Clutch fully squeezed = 0 percent power to the wheel. Remember, squeezing the clutch is the same as shutting the engine off—any time you get into trouble, cut power to the rear wheel by squeezing the clutch.

Clutch fully released = 100 percent power to the wheel, bike is now controlled with throttle grip.

Somewhere between fully squeezed and fully released lies the ever-elusive friction point—the point at which the engine starts to send power to the rear wheel. When you feel it, hold it there and ease the clutch out even more gently to keep your starts smooth.

The whole process from 0 percent to 100 percent should take you at least ten seconds when you're first learning. With a day of practice, you should have it down to about five seconds, and by the time you have about 500 miles under your belt, it should take no more than a few seconds.

If you made the rookie mistake of buying a 600-cc or bigger sportbike for your first bike, when you head for that cornfield you'll probably be doing it on one wheel!

Lugging: Using the clutch, brakes, or inertia to lower the engine rpm almost to the point of stalling.

Braking Situation	Brake Use (%)							
Normal Stopping	0		30		50		30	10
Emergency Stopping	0	10	40	**80**	**90**	**100**	50	10
Normal Slowing	0		10	20	30		10	0
Emergency Slowing	0		10	30	60		30	10

These percentages are only guidelines for mental practice: every bike and every actual stop will be a little different. Notice that in all cases, braking starts at 10% power—don't grab too quickly. In normal cases it does not go above 50%. Also note that braking pressure always builds up then backs off. Practice these four situations in your garage with the bike turned off. Get a feel for the brake lever and visualize the situations and pressures you'll need to use them smoothly.

In normal stopping situations, squeeze the brake the same way you'd give a light, firm handshake—enough to introduce yourself, but not so much that you could crush a steel can or seem, well, too eager to introduce yourself.

Right Hand: Using the Front Brake
On the other side of the handlebars you'll find the front brake lever. It looks just like the clutch lever and, on most bikes, controls 75 percent or more of the bike's stopping power, so get comfortable with it before moving on to any other controls. The front brake works by clamping down on the front wheel to slow the bike. While you're learning, it'll be easy to accidentally clamp down too hard or too fast and stall or destabilize the bike, but there are a couple of tricks to keep you smooth.

In normal stopping situations, squeeze the brake the same way you'd give a *light, firm* handshake—enough to introduce yourself, but not so much that you could crush a steel can or seem, well, *too* eager to introduce yourself. The front brake requires only a light touch and some finesse, and riders rarely need to squeeze the lever more than halfway in normal situations. The other key to mastering the front brake is to start with a light touch and squeeze progressively harder—don't "grab" too quickly. You can't go from 0 percent to 100 percent (like the clutch) with one squeeze; you need to work your way up, adding pressure as you go: 0 percent, 10 percent, 30 percent, and 50 percent (halfway) in normal situations.

Turning
The handlebars are used to lean the bike and to point it in the direction you want to go. Don't hang on to the bike and the bars

If you've spent any time on a bicycle, you already know intuitively how to steer a motorcycle. They're both two-wheeled, single-track vehicles and they both adhere to the same laws of physics. Both require countersteering, but because a motorcycle is about 10-20 times heavier than a bicycle, the inputs you need to give it are more obvious.

Countersteering: Turning the handlebars to the left to make the bike lean to the right, and vice versa; pressing forward on the left handgrip (pointing the front tire to the right) to initiate a left turn, and vice versa.

with a death grip by tensing up your hands, arms, and shoulders. Hold the handlebars lightly—again, like a light handshake. Use the handlebars to guide the bike, not to keep yourself from falling off. (See "proper posture" later in this chapter.)

One of the wonderful mysteries of motorcycling is countersteering. Up to four or five miles per hour, your motorcycle will feel like a bicycle, but after that something magical happens. It feels like something else—a motorcycle!

At *very* slow speeds, you use the handlebars to point the front tire in the direction you want to go. If you want the bike to go right, you point the tire to the right and away you go. If you want to go left, it's the same deal: point it and shoot.

However, once you get into higher speeds (more than 5 miles per hour or so) the bike needs to be *leaned* before it can be *turned*. (This is the case with bicycles too, but because they weigh less than one-tenth of a motorcycle, it's not as noticeable.) To lean the motorcycle, turn the handlebars and point the tire in the *opposite* direction you want to go. That is, if you want the bike to go right, you have to first point the tire left by pressing forward on the *right* handgrip—this leans the bike to the right and the tire then points naturally into the turn. If you want to go left, turn the handlebars and tire to the right first by pressing forward on the *left* handgrip to lean the bike, then as the bike leans over to the left the handlebars and tire will point left and the bike will go left.

This sounds a lot more complicated than it really is, so it's best to just not think about it. On a motorcycle, you're rarely going less than 5 miles per hour, so when you want to turn, always use countersteering to turn the bike: to go right, turn *left*, lean *right*, and go right. To go left, turn *right*, lean *left*, and go left. Once you've tried this a couple of times it will all make sense.

Newbie: Experienced riders' affectionate term for a NEW, BEginning rider. Sometimes written as "nube."

On the other hand, you've got those riders out there with a few hundred street miles under their belts, all taken brazenly at 30–70 miles per hour or more, who have found out that a bike at that speed seems stable and easy to control. They think they've got it figured out. That's great for them, until they try to force their great big bike through a maze of little cones and lines at 5–15 miles per hour in front of an examiner. All of the sudden they feel like a fish out of water.

While you're first learning, you have to temporarily suspend the logical part of your brain that says to take it really, really slow. Taking it slow is the wrong thing to do. You have to take it fast. Not *fast*-fast, but fast enough to get the wheels turning so they help balance the bike: 7–10 miles per hour at least. (To do this safely, you have to practice in an area where there is plenty of room and no obstructions like cars, curbs, light poles, and trees.) Once you've turned a few miles and have your confidence and smile built up, you can start gradually reducing your speeds—6, 5, 4 miles per hour—and so on, deliberately challenging yourself until you've mastered both a stable and unstable motorcycle. Controlling the bike at low speeds requires a great deal of skill, which will pay off when it comes time to demonstrate that skill in front of an instructor or examiner.

Too many riders are victims of overconfidence and never learn low-speed maneuvering. These riders fail their skill tests miserably and complain that little cones and slow speeds are not realistic. (No, but the skills being measured are.)

While you're first learning, you have to temporarily suspend the logical part of your brain that says to take it really, really slow. You have to take it fast. Not fast-fast, but fast enough to get the wheels turning so their movement helps balance the bike.

Big Secret Number 3: Stability

Except when parked properly (in gear, sidestand down, handlebars turned full-lock left) or tipped over in a driveway or parking lot somewhere, a motorcycle is most stable—that is, resistant to change—when it's moving. And the faster it's moving, the more stable it is. At very high speeds, a motorcycle is probably more stable than when it's parked. There are lots of complicated reasons for this, but it boils down to the fact that the spinning wheels of a bike create a gyroscopic effect that makes the bike behave like . . . well, like a bike should behave.

This is a scary point that's tough for beginner motorcyclists to swallow. And it's a frustrating reality for novice motorcyclists who *think* they're experienced motorcyclists, or at least those who think they're experienced enough to pass the test to earn their motorcycle license.

At slow speeds (1–6 miles per hour or so), a motorcycle is very unstable. It's jerky, wobbly, bouncy, and seems to want to fall over every time you turn the handlebars or squeeze the brake. Even up to 10 miles per hour, the bike still doesn't feel as if it wants to go where you point it and stop where you want it to. This is what makes learning to ride a motorcycle such a challenge and the first few miles so dangerous. It's natural to take everything slow, but taking everything slow makes it harder to learn! Take it slow and easy and the bike behaves like you're trying to ride a great big dog.

At slow speeds, a motorcycle is very unstable. It's jerky, wobbly, bouncy, and seems to want to fall over every time you turn the handlebars or squeeze the brake.

Gear	Speed	Upshift	Downshift
1	0-10 mph	10 mph	
2	5-25 mph	25 mph	5 mph
3	20-40 mph	45 mph	20 mph
4	35-55 mph	55 mph	35 mph
5	55+ mph		50 mph

Every bike will be different, but here are some basic guidelines for when to upshift (when accelerating) and downshift (when slowing) to keep the engine spinning in the desired rpm range. Another easy way to judge shift points is to shift at a certain rpm range—check your owner's manual or performance specs to find the middle of your powerband, which would be your ideal shift point.

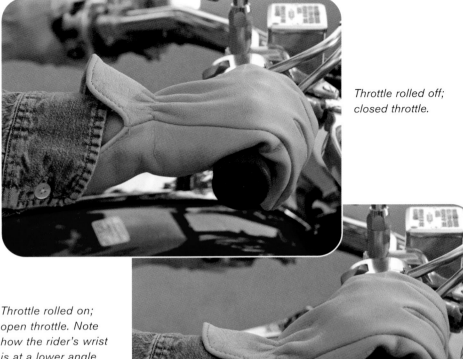

Throttle rolled off; closed throttle.

Throttle rolled on; open throttle. Note how the rider's wrist is at a lower angle than the forearm or throttle grip: this is the "wrist-down" position.

Just as you learned in driver's ed to use the same foot for both gas pedal and brake, the right hand either uses the throttle or the brake on a motorcycle— not both at once.

Controlling Your Speed

Okay, you're able to go, stop, and turn, using the clutch, front brake, and handlebars. Now it's time to dig into the finer points of controlling the bike. First we'll start with throttle management.

You're on a Roll Now

The throttle mechanism is the right handgrip itself, and it works just like the gas pedal of a car—except you're also using that hand to help steer the bike. To give the bike more gas and make it go faster, you rotate the grip toward you. This is rolling it *on*. To give the bike less gas and slow it down, turn the grip away from you. This is rolling it *off*. This is also sometimes referred to as *opening* (rolling it on) and *closing* (rolling it off) the throttle.

The resting position for the throttle is off—a spring keeps it rolled completely closed. When you first use the throttle grip, you'll only be able to move it one direction: toward you. When you let go of the throttle grip, the spring automatically snaps the throttle closed.

Being located very close to the front brake makes it tough to use the front brake and the throttle at the same time. Just as you learned in driver's ed to use the same foot for both gas pedal and brake, the right hand either uses the throttle or the brake on a motorcycle—not both at once.

The Subtler Speed Controls: Shifting and Using the Rear Brake

The clutch, front brake, throttle, and handlebars do almost everything you could ever want to do on a motorcycle: stop, go, and turn. But what if you want to make finer adjustments, such as managing engine speed or increasing your braking effectiveness? A bike wouldn't last long driven every day in first gear only. And there's a wheel and tire on the back of the bike that can be employed to help stop the bike—or keep it stationary while you're using your hands to work the throttle and clutch.

The Shift Lever

Probably the most feared and hardest to learn of all motorcycle operations, shifting gears is actually very simple. At your left foot there's a lever. Squeeze the clutch and roll off the throttle, lift it up on the lever with your toe one click, and smoothly release the clutch and roll on the throttle, and you've just shifted up one gear. Clutch and throttle, press down with your toe one click, clutch and throttle, and you've just downshifted one gear.

Your bike will have four to six gears. By nature, the bike is always in gear. A "neutral" position, kind of midway between first gear and second gear, is easiest to find with the bike stopped and the engine running. Put the bike in neutral only when parking on level surfaces, warming it up in the morning, or when you need to give your clutch hand a rest. You'll rarely need to put the bike in neutral when riding.

Timing is the hardest thing to learn when shifting—sometimes the bike "wants" to shift and sometimes it doesn't. (Stubborn little buggers, sometimes.) Your goal when shifting and selecting a gear is to keep your engine running in a desired rpm range—generally, at the bottom of the powerband. Only shift when you need to shift. If you shift too early, your bike will not have spun up to the desired range yet, and it will resist the shift or lug the engine. If you shift too late, the bike will want to "slam" into gear and scream in protest. If you're having trouble shifting, it's probably not your technique but your timing.

If you're having trouble shifting, it's probably not your technique but your timing.

Powerband: An area in the rpm range where a motorcycle makes maximum power due to engine design and fuel combustion rate (octane).

Rear Brake

The rear brake is a complement to the front brake, and should only rarely be used by itself. In fact, consider the rear brake an accessory: It's there for convenience, but you can pretty much live without it. It's there to make you ride *better*. It's not as powerful as the front brake, but is useful for making minor speed adjustments and to hold the bike still at stoplights or on hills. It's also useful in emergency situations when you need your bike to make every effort to slow down, and it's especially good in situations of low traction (loose gravel, slippery pavement, ice cream on the sidewalk) where you might want to avoid using the front brake. It's also a good way to appear as if you're marching to some unheard drummer while you tap the brake at a stoplight. No matter how you look at it, it's one of the main controls, so it's a good habit to get used to using both brakes at the same time.

The Peripheral Controls

At your right thumb there is a red switch—the engine cut-off, or "kill" switch. This works exactly like the ignition key in that it cuts the power to the engine, except you're able to use it without removing your hands from the handlebars.

Somewhere there'll be a choke mechanism (unless you sprang for a fuel-injected bike). Use this to start the bike when the engine is cold, "choking" off the bike's air supply, allowing it to start easier. Be careful not to leave the choke on too long—just long enough to warm up the motor a little—or it will cause the bike to run too rich and start "choking" the spark plugs and combustion process with too much fuel.

The turn signals are located at your left thumb, and have three positions: left, right, and off. Some of the more investment-intensive bikes ($$$) have fancy buttons at each grip for the signals. Your signals normally won't self-cancel, so you'll have to use the switch twice every time you use your signals: once to start the signal blinking and once to stop it. To use the signal, slide it either left or right. To stop the signal from blinking, either slide the switch back to center or press it, depending on the bike.

Your lights and horn are also at your left thumb. Your headlight should always be on, so your only job is to decide whether to use high or low beam. Your horn is a great tool to draw attention to yourself, but don't rely too heavily on it—imagine a baby duck with a sweat sock stuffed in its mouth, that's what a typical motorcycle horn sounds like. The starter button is at your right thumb beneath the kill switch. If your bike has a kick starter, it's usually on the right side behind the engine. To use the kick starter, don't think of yourself as "kicking" the engine to life, but rather use the kick starter as a crank to "spin" the engine to life.

Pulling It All Together

Your ability to work all these controls while simultaneously keeping an eye on the road and traffic is the ultimate juggling act. Just like golfing, playing piano, or attracting a mate, all your body parts have to play their respective positions (like football players on a gridiron) in order for you to have a snowball's chance of getting the job done. It's not easy, and it doesn't come all at once. Take it slow and enjoy the experience.

Be careful not to leave the choke on too long—just long enough to warm up the motor a little—or it will cause the bike to run too rich and start "choking" the spark plugs and combustion process with too much fuel.

A motorcycle rider uses his or her whole body to ride smoothly and skillfully. As a beginner, you'll have the urge to hold onto the bike by the handlebars, especially when you get tired. Don't do that. Quit for the day if you're too tired to hold on with your legs. It takes a while to build up that lower muscle "clamping" strength. Your best riding will come when you're holding on with your lower body, and your upper body is relaxed and ready to react at a moment's notice.

What People Say and What People Mean Number 3: "Look Down, Go Down"

"Look down, go down" is the old-school phrase of riders trying to impress you with their arcane knowledge of motorcycle fundamentals. They're trying to say, "If you stare at the ground, you'll crash," and it's true, in a backward sort of way. "You go where you look" is a better way to say it—and the mantra of MSF coaches and students. And it works. The simplest and most elusive motorcycle control technique is to *use your head and eyes to control the bike*.

But wait—don't your hands control the bike? Do you really go where you look? How is that possible? If I look down, will I go down?

Gymnasts, high divers, and acrobats all use this technique—by focusing your head in the "direction" of the desired result, your body will want to follow. It works the same way on a motorcycle. By focusing your eyes and the orientation of your head in the direction you want your bike to go, you're making it that much easier for your body (and bike) to do what you want it to do.

Put it this way: If you're focused completely on the road ahead of you, it would take nearly an act of God to send you off the road and into, say, the broad side of a barn. On the other hand, if you decide to focus on the roadside bushes, it's going to take nearly an act of God to keep you from doing some unplanned landscaping. This is what's known as "target fixation," when your mind focuses on a target—intended or unintended—and you ride right into it because you're mentally incapable of making your bike go anywhere else.

The bike doesn't necessarily "go where you look," but it's almost impossible for a new rider to make a bike go somewhere he or she is not looking. The best way to say it would be, "You can't make the bike go to a place that you're not looking," but that takes a lot longer to say and it's not quite as catchy.

Don't leave your driveway without a quick review of good posture.

Just before a turn, focus your head and eyes on the place you want your bike to be in three to four seconds. Keep your eyes there until you've apexed the turn, then move your eyes another three to four seconds ahead.

Posture Perfect

Smart motorcyclists ride with their shoulders relaxed, arms loose, a light, firm grip on the handlebars, back straight, knees pressed tightly against the motorcycle, balls of their feet on the footpegs, and head up and eyes looking toward the horizon. Go through a checklist every time you ride: shoulders, arms, hands, back, knees, feet, head, and eyes. Don't leave your driveway without a quick review of good posture.

Apex: The point when cornering where you are closest to the inside of the turn; in a right turn, the point when you are closest to the right edge, and vice versa.

Target Fixation: The phenomenon when a motorcyclist consciously or unconsciously stares at an area or object, unintentionally forcing the bike to go in that direction.

Armchair Motorcyclist

Until you've completed the MSF basic course, the best place to practice using the controls is in your garage or driveway with the bike turned OFF. In fact, even before that, it's best that you practice these next six techniques from the place you're reading right now, then go practice them with the bike off. Study the following exercises, imagine yourself on your bike, and go through the motions. Get an idea of what it will be like before you ever try it on a real bike.

Try some armchair motorcycling: Visualize yourself riding smoothly and skillfully, using proper posture and precise control, before you get out there and mix it up with traffic. This will help you physically, mentally, and emotionally as a beginner and any time you're learning something new—whatever you're trying to learn will be already somewhat familiar to you because you will have practiced it in your mind.

Exercise 1: Starting from a Stop

With your head and eyes looking well ahead, both feet on the ground, you're

If I look down, will I go down?

Try some armchair motorcycling: Visualize yourself riding smoothly and skillfully, using proper posture and precise control, before you get out there and mix it up with traffic.

going to squeeze the clutch, press the shift lever to find first gear, then smoothly ease out the clutch about halfway until you feel the friction point. The bike wants to pull you forward, but don't do anything yet. Hold the bike in place with your feet, keep the clutch right where it is, and open the throttle slightly. Hear the engine rev up a little bit. Now, ease the clutch out just a little farther. The engine revs will go back down, and the bike is pulling harder. Now it's time to get moving. Open up the throttle a little more, hear the engine rev, and smoothly ease the clutch farther into the friction zone, and opening the throttle as you do. Imagine the bike pulling smoothly and strongly out onto the road. As soon as the bike is stable (at about 5 miles per hour) put your feet on the footpegs, grip the bike with your knees and legs, and relax your arms and shoulders and keep accelerating up to about 10 miles per hour.

IMPORTANT NOTE: Remember Big Secret Number 3! At very slow speeds, the bike is not stable. Don't waste too much time below 5 miles per hour. (If you want to go that slow, take a hike, buddy!) Once you've released the clutch, gently but firmly accelerate up to at least 10 miles per hour or so. It's okay—don't panic. If you get spooked you can always squeeze the clutch to cut power to the engine, but wobbling around at walking speed is a sure-fire way to tip over, hit a curb, or introduce Mr. Front Tire to Ms. Angry Neighbor's Car.

Exercise 2: Stopping Smoothly

You've got the bike moving in first gear; now imagine you're going to come to a smooth stop at a stop sign. Roll off the throttle and squeeze the clutch, disengaging the engine. Now you're coasting with the engine running at idle. Gently squeeze the front brake with your right hand and press the rear brake with your right foot. When you feel the bike

Using your legs to hold the bike in place while releasing the clutch with your hand will help you learn to modulate the clutch and throttle.

start to slow, squeeze and press the brakes a little more to control exactly how and where the bike comes to a stop. Modulate your braking so you stop with your front tire even with the stop sign. Once you're stopped, you should have your left foot on the ground, your right foot on the rear brake, the clutch squeezed, and the engine running, and the bike should be in first gear. Put your fingers back on the throttle, and you're ready try exercise one again.

Important note: Don't come to a complete stop unless your bike is straight up and down and the handlebars and front tire are pointing straight ahead. Stopping while leaned over, even slightly, is a foolproof recipe for falling over sideways at the first stop sign.

Modulation: Subtly increasing, decreasing, or varying the input (squeezing, pressing, or rolling on/off) for precise control and positioning of motorcycle.

Idle Speed: The low speed (750–1,500 rpm) at which an engine runs with the clutch disengaged and without any throttle input from the rider.

At very slow speeds, the bike is not stable. Don't waste too much time below 5 miles per hour.

Entry Speed: The speed at which the rider can safely negotiate a corner while rolling on the throttle throughout the turn.

The bike will feel most stable in the turn if you gently roll on the throttle while you're turning.

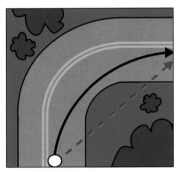

The black line is the bike's path of travel. The red line is your initial head turn/line of sight: two to four seconds ahead. Note that the black bike line does not follow the curve radius, but instead starts toward the outside of the turn, clips the inside at the middle, and finishes on the outside. This path of travel effectively widens the turn and allows for safer cornering. You'll use the "outside-inside-outside" technique for the rest of your motorcycle days, so start getting used to the idea now.

Exercise 3: Turning at Slow Speed–Slow, Roll, Look, Press

Once you've mastered mentally starting and stopping, it's time to go around the block. Imagine your neighborhood with no stop signs and everybody's out of town for the weekend, so there is no traffic.

Get the bike moving smoothly in a straight line and head for the first right turn at about 10 miles per hour. As you approach the corner, decelerate to about 8 miles per hour by closing the throttle slightly, and move to the left of your lane ("slow"). Once you're in position and at entry speed, open the throttle again slightly ("roll"). Turn your head and look through the turn two to four seconds ahead ("look"). Countersteer—turn the handlebars to the left by pressing forward on the right handgrip ("press"). This will lean the bike to the right. Now gently open the throttle and make a smooth right turn onto the next street. Ride down that street until the next right turn, and then do it again. Keep making right turns until you end up back at your driveway. Then, turn your bike around and do the whole thing to the left. Keep imagining smooth turns, gently accelerating and looking well ahead, all the while keeping the bike in first gear at about 10 miles per hour.

The bike will feel most stable in the turn if you gently roll on the throttle *while* you're turning. Just before you turn your head, open the throttle slightly, then

look through the turn and press the handgrip to countersteer the bike.

Important note: This four-step cornering process—slow, roll, look, and press—differs from the one you'll learn in the MSF course (see Chapter 4), which uses "slow, look, press, and roll." Don't let the difference confuse you. Just pick one and stick to it. Your own riding technique will eventually differ slightly from both of them. Most important is that your head is turned before the bike is turned.

Exercise 4: Accelerating and Upshifting

Pretty soon you're going to get bored riding around your imaginary neighborhood at 10 miles per hour. It's time to start practicing some shifting. Between stop signs or turns, shift up twice to third gear.

Get the bike moving and stable in a straight line. Accelerate quickly up to 10 miles per hour. You'll hear the engine wind up into the revs. Smoothly and quickly roll off the throttle and squeeze the clutch at the same time. You'll now be coasting at about 10 miles per hour. Lift up once, firmly, on the shift lever, then ease out the clutch and gently roll on the throttle. You're now in second gear. Accelerate again, this time up to about 25 miles per hour, and then do it again: roll off, squeeze clutch, lift up, ease out, and roll on. You're now in third gear. Gently accelerate and level out at about 30 miles per hour.

Motorcycles are designed to handle properly when the throttle is opened. Resist the temptation to slow down during a turn. Slow down before the turn, then open the throttle and smoothly and gently accelerate all the way through the turn. Talk yourself through it: slow, roll, look, press.

While you're learning, it's easiest to shift at certain points on the speedometer. After several hours of practice, you'll start to shift based on the way the engine sounds. When that happens, you will have just made another leap in your evolution as a motorcyclist.

Engine Braking: Slowing a motorcycle with the rear wheel by rolling off the throttle and/or downshifting.

IMPORTANT NOTE: The bike won't want to shift if you're not accelerating. Resist the temptation to shift too early—there's no reason to be in third gear at 10 miles per hour, and the bike won't like it. The bike will shift much more easily when the revs are up.

Exercise 5: Slowing (or Stopping) and Downshifting

As you approach a corner or a stop, you'll need to get the bike slowed down again and in the right gear. Roll off the throttle, let the bike slow to about 20 miles per hour, squeeze the clutch, press the shift lever down one click, and then gently ease out the clutch, opening the throttle just slightly. You're now back into second gear. Apply both brakes with the clutch released and the bike in gear to slow further.

If you're coming up to a corner and don't intend to stop, allow the engine and bike to wind down to your entry speed (8–10 miles per hour) in second gear, then open the throttle slightly, look through the turn, press on the handgrip, and away you go!

If you're in third gear and coming to a stop, the technique is a little different. Roll off the throttle and squeeze the clutch at the same time. Apply both brakes. When you get to about 20 miles per hour, press the shift lever down one click without releasing the clutch. You're now in second gear. When you get down to about 5 miles per hour, press the shift lever again without releasing the clutch. You're now in first gear and ready to go again after you've completed your stop.

Important note: By keeping the clutch squeezed as you come to a stop allows the brakes to do most of the work of stopping. In real life, this is good, because the brake light will alert others to your intentions better than engine braking. Lots of mouth-breathers out there think braking with the clutch (engine braking) is cool, but the reality is, unless you're a factory-sponsored racer, brake pads are simpler to replace than clutch pads. Use engine braking for special occasions, not for everyday work.

The bike will feel most stable in the turn if you gently roll on the throttle while you're turning.

The Basic Nuts and Bolts–Keeping Your Motorcycle Running Right

It's okay to keep a dirty motorcycle (it shows you spend more time riding it than putzing with it!), but cleaning it regularly can alert you to potential problems before they become severe. Keep your motorcycle clean by washing with soapy water and an old rag. Dishsoap or car-cleaning products (I prefer Zip Wax) work fine, but be careful not to drown electrical wiring or components. Try not to overdo it on your gauges or chain. For tough grease and road oil and grime, a clean rag moistened with mineral spirits or brake cleaner usually cuts it without damaging the surface, but be sure to wash those areas—and your hands—again with soap and water. Dry the bike with a clean, old towel. Only spray or slosh water on the bike when it's cool—a hot engine or parts can be damaged if soaked in cold water from the hose.

Whaddya Mean *Tools*?

You're going to need a few tools to perform basic maintenance. It's okay to start with inexpensive tools, but you're smartest to buy good ones that will last a lifetime—they'll be like new and work properly when you need them. You should include these items in the cost of your motorcycle.

Get a good tire pressure gauge, utility knife (razor blade), latex gloves, WD-40, brake cleaner, hand cleaner, and chain lube at the bare-bones minimum. Most maintenance and repairs you can do using the owner's manual, but buying a shop manual for your bike pays off in the long run. Start saving old T-shirts and towels for shop rags.

Buy a 3/8-inch ratchet and metric sockets from 7 to 19 millimeters. If your bike uses standard-sized nuts and bolts,

get a standard socket set too. It's handy to have one or two socket extensions and a universal socket joint. Someday you'll find use for both 1/4-inch and 1/2-inch drivers and sockets, too, but you can get by with 3/8 for now.

Find a 3/8-inch torque wrench that measures in both SAE and metric values. Motorcycles are engineered precisely and require exact inputs when tightening nuts and bolts. A torque wrench can help you seat your fasteners properly and keep you from breaking bolts when you get too . . . well . . . energetic. Start with a torque wrench that can measure from 20 to 100 ft-lb.

Get a good combination wrench set and a ball-end Allen-wrench set. Sockets are fun and clicky, but for the real work you need a quality wrench that fits exactly in or on the bolt you're trying to adjust.

Buy three different sizes each of both flathead and Phillips screwdrivers: small, medium, and large. It's not a bad idea to splurge on a couple of medium-sized shorties, too, for those tight spaces. Pick up a cheap set of tiny electronics/jeweler screwdrivers for the various itty-bitty fasteners you'll inevitably have to deal with.

Buy extras of your most commonly used tools and keep them on the bike in a little pouch—a homemade tool kit for emergency repairs on the road. There's typically enough room under the seat to store the kit on the bike.

Adjusting the Controls

The brake and clutch lever angles, hand-grip locations, handlebar angle and height, shift lever height, brake pedal height, and mirror positions are all adjustable to some degree. Take some time when you first buy your motorcycle

Most maintenance and repairs you can do using the owner's manual, but buying a shop manual for your bike pays off in the long run.

At a minimum, this is your tool kit: regular and needle-nose pliers, regular and Phillips-head screwdrivers (a shorty or two is advisable), tire gauge, utility knife, Allen wrenches, WD-40, combination wrenches, socket wrenches and sockets, a torque wrench, and some mechanic's gloves. Mark tools you use a lot with colored duct tape for easier identification.

to get a feel for where the controls are, and use your new tools to get them into the exact positions that you want them. Your goal is to put the controls into positions in which they are comfortable and natural for you to use. Some bikes come from the factory with knobs or dials you can turn to tweak the controls to your liking. Otherwise, it's a matter of loosening up the bolts that hold them on, moving them around, and tightening them back up again. Use WD-40 to lubricate the insides of the clutch and throttle cables and any pivot points where the controls, including the footrests and sidestand, move.

Some bikes come from the factory with knobs or dials you can turn to tweak the controls to your liking.

Once the pad material wears down to the backing plate, the brakes will start grinding away at the rotor and destroy it. A $30 set of brake pads is a lot cheaper than a $200 rotor, so don't let it come to that.

Your brakes should give good, firm feedback when squeezed or pressed.

Safety Check

Check the pressure and condition of the tires before every ride, or at the very least once a week. Refer to the owner's manual for tire pressure, and check and set the pressure when the tires are cold. The tires should have good tread, no cracks or blue coloring on the sidewalls, and be free of anything stuck in the treads.

Take a peek at the engine oil and add as needed. Use only motorcycle-specific oil because the engine and transmission usually share this oil and normal automotive oil doesn't hold up. Plan on changing the oil every 3,000 miles, more often if you store the bike for the winter or only take short rides, less often if you ride year-round and regularly run the bike at highway speeds for 100 miles or more at a time.

Your brakes should give good, firm feedback when squeezed or pressed. They should both be slightly "loose." (This is called free play.) Check the brake pads monthly—you should have at least 3 millimeters of pad life left—about the thickness of a house key. Sometimes it's tricky to see the pads with the brake calipers mounted on the bike—you may have to remove them to check properly. If they're nearly worn to the backing plate, or when they start to squeal or grind, it's time for a brake job.

If you have hydraulic brakes (or clutch), bleed them and replace the fluid once per year. Refer to your shop manual for bleeding instructions.

The throttle grip should have a little free play and snap back to the closed position when rolled on and released. Refer to the owner's manual or shop manual for adjusting the throttle grip.

The clutch should have a little free play and give good feedback when squeezed. The friction point should be about halfway through the lever's travel. Refer to the owner's manual or shop manual to adjust the clutch.

The suspension should travel freely—bounce the motorcycle, watch, and listen for problems. On many bikes, suspension is adjustable—you can adjust the way it feels (hardness or softness) and the way it reacts to bumps. Refer to the owner's manual or shop manual.

The chain should be clean, lubricated, and droop just a little. You should be able to move the bottom of the chain (midway between the front and rear sprockets) up and down about 3/4 of an inch. If it's too tight or too loose, you'll need to adjust it. Essentially, all it involves is loosening the rear wheel, turning a couple of adjusting bolts, and tightening it back up. Refer to the owner's manual or shop manual.

Recommended Reading:

The Motorcycle Safety Foundation's Guide to Motorcycling Excellence: A well-renowned and solid book full of photos and diagrams covering all the important basics.

101 Sportbike Performance Projects by Evans Brasfield—While focusing on only one type of bike, the author delivers step-by-step motorcycle care and maintenance information that *anyone* with *any* type of bike can use.

Free Play: The degree of "looseness" in a motorcycle hand or foot control lever; the amount the control needs to be squeezed, pressed, or turned before it actually begins to engage the control. The throttle, brake levers, clutch, and shift lever require at least 1/8–1/4 inch of free play for smooth operation and longevity.

Bleeding: Removing unwanted air or old fluid from a hydraulic brake or clutch system.

Use only motorcycle-specific oil because the engine and transmission usually share this oil and normal automotive oil doesn't hold up.

GETTING SKILLED

ARMED WITH THE BASICS OF MOTORCYCLE OPERATION AND MAINTENANCE, YOU'RE READY TO START RIDING. AS WITH EVERYTHING MOTORCYCLE, THERE'S MORE TO IT THAN MEETS THE EYE.

The smartest way to learn to ride is to turn yourself over to the experts. The Motorcycle Safety Foundation (MSF) is there to get you over the first few hurdles without the inordinate risk and drama of learning on the street—its basic rider course (BRC) is the best way to get your feet wet in the world of motorcycling. But the BRC is not the end-all; it is only the very beginning. Once you've dipped your toes, you've got more work to do before you're skilled enough even to deal with traffic.

To ride safely and with confidence requires months, even years, of dedicated practice and discovery. Don't be a butthead and try to skip steps in the process. Everything worth doing is worth taking the time to do it right. Skipping steps is cheating yourself of hard-earned victories and those glorious moments of epiphany—the light bulb suddenly going on over your head—so when you do finally take the course you'll end up saying to yourself, "Why didn't I do this 20 years ago? I've been doing it *wrong* the whole time!"

During your first five or six months learning to ride a motorcycle, you are at great risk of death and injury. Spending a couple of days learning from experienced coaches away from traffic will get you through your first 100 or so awkward miles in relative safety. And it will leave you with the tools you need to strike out on your own. If you ignored my advice in Chapter 3 and have already gone out and practiced on your own, you'll be amazed at how much you still don't know.

In this chapter I'm going to shed some light on exactly what's involved in motorcycle training, clarify what you should expect to get from it, and show you how to use what you learn to start the process of developing into a true, skilled motorcyclist. I'll also provide specific guidelines, strategies, and practice tips you'll need to build to get your license.

Get the Wheels Turning

Harry Hurt found in 1981 that most riders involved in crashes hadn't had any formal training at all—most were self-taught, or learned at the hands of a friend or family member. Soon after, the MSF rolled out its program to correct the situation. This early incarnation of today's BRC was meant to teach riders the basics of safe riding: preparation, street strategy, and the seemingly unattainable skills of emergency braking, countersteering, and swerving. Untrained riders just didn't know about that stuff.

Harry Hurt: The pioneer in motorcycle safety research who authored the landmark 1981 study *Motorcycle Accident Cause Factors and Identification of Countermeasures*, a.k.a. the "Hurt Study."

Today's basic training has 20-plus years of research, field-testing, and educational theory behind it, and is a short and sweet way to go from wobbly tourist to road-hungry newbie in about 15 hours. And it's more than that: The BRC is a promotional device for the motorcycle industry, putting a safe and smiling face on motorcycling and removing some of the barriers to getting started. Nearly every state has a program that uses the MSF curriculum to train new riders. Many of these programs provide training bikes as part of the program. The cost is inexpensive ($100–300) for 5 hours of classroom instruction, 10 hours of practice on their motorcycle, and two coaches giving you quality feedback! What a bargain! In most states, completing the course will allow you to skip steps in the licensing process, usually the skill test. These reasons alone are enough to take the course.

Why Training Is Critical

Riding a motorcycle may look easy, but there is a lot more to it than most people realize. The risks involved may not be apparent to someone who's been safe and secure in a four-wheeled cage all their life. Riders need to employ defensive strategies—approaches to driving and traffic that are absolutely critical to survival—that require a real attitude adjustment. And skills like visual directional control, emergency braking, countersteering, traction management, and swerving are very difficult for riders to learn on their own—without at least some guidance. Think of the MSF basic course as the tour guide in iceberg town.

No matter how badly you want to get on your motorcycle, no matter how long the wait for a BRC, no matter how much fun your friends are having on *their* motorcycles, don't try to learn on your own bike without first taking the BRC. There is simply no valid reason to skip this step. And if you've already begun riding without taking the BRC, slow down! Sign up for the next available class and be very careful about the situations in which you put yourself until you have completed the course. There's simply too much that you don't know yet.

No matter how badly you want to get on your motorcycle, no matter how long the wait for a BRC, no matter how much fun your friends are having on their motorcycles, don't try to learn on your own bike without first taking the BRC.

Where to Go, What You'll Need

Call the MSF toll-free at 800-446-9227 or visit www.msf-usa.org for a directory of state and local training programs. Most states—though not all—have a program in place, and in many states the demand for training outstrips the supply, so don't be surprised if you have to wait or travel a fair distance to find a course. Don't worry—it'll be worth it.

Bring your driver's license, motorcycle permit (if you have one), and riding gear to the class. You'll be required to cover all your exposed skin with a DOT-approved helmet, eye protection, long pants, long sleeves, full-fingered gloves, and over-the-ankle footwear. Bring a smile, too, because you're about to have the most fun you've ever had.

Bring a few note cards and a pencil. As you proceed through the riding exercises,

make notes to yourself on what is working, what isn't, what you like, what you don't, what you're having trouble with, and what comes easily. You'll refer to these notes later, so hold on to them.

What You'll Do

You'll spend some time in the classroom working to unlock the mental side of motorcycling. Reading, video presentations, and group discussions will help prepare you for the on-cycle riding exercises and common situations you'll deal with in the real world.

Then you'll move on to the parking lot for a couple of days of intense structured practice. The pace moves quickly. Starting from the very basics of learning the motorcycle controls, you'll start grinding away at your lack of motorcycle knowledge and skills. By the end of the

Bring a smile, too, because you're about to have the most fun you've ever had.

Both riders have the gear they need to take the BRC. Only one rider has gear good enough for street riding. You can get by with street clothes for the purposes of training (on a closed-off parking lot, away from traffic, doing specific drills, and supervised) but don't assume this minimum requirement means it's safe to wear this crap on the street.

first day, you'll be a different person. You'll be as exhausted as a rented mule. You'll feel like you've learned everything you can possibly learn about motorcycling—but you have learned just the basics. On the second day you'll learn all the important stuff, the tricky stuff, the stuff you couldn't have learned on your own in a million years—the stuff that can save your life someday. Even veteran riders (old dogs) who finally take the basic course learn some new tricks.

Each practice drill starts with clear, concise instructions. The instructors will demonstrate the exercise first so you can visualize what you're about to do, and they'll narrate along the way so you understand what skill(s) you'll be working on and why. Then you'll have 15–30 minutes to practice the drill, and a

quick debriefing after it's over. Then you're on to the next one.

What's really cool about the BRC is that its structure is so scientific, so purposeful, that you learn on both conscious and unconscious levels. While you're concentrating on one particular skill—for example, starting and stopping—the exercise is laid out in such a way that you learn how to turn without realizing it. Then when the time comes to actually practice turning, you will have already built many of those skills without knowing it, the process will be safer and more fun, and the joy of overcoming challenges will come easier. Many detractors say that the BRC is not thorough enough, at least compared to the old version. Turns out it's a lot more thorough than it appears, just more subtle in its approach.

What's really cool about the BRC is that its structure is so scientific, so purposeful, that you learn on both conscious and unconscious levels.

The instructors, called "rider coaches," know exactly what to say, how to say it, and when to say it to give you the best retention and learning experience. They'll walk you through every facet of motorcycle operation, then give you time to practice on your own—but will always be at the ready when you have a question or need additional help.

Big Secret Number 4:
"What You Really Get from an MSF Basic Course"

Don't be lured into the trap of thinking you're a good rider when you're not. Just because you passed the BRC, grew more in two days than you ever have in your life, and learned more than you ever thought possible, you're still only at the beginning. There's a lot more to do before you can even call yourself a motorcyclist.

At this point you should compare motorcycling to playing the piano. If you took a crash course (no pun intended) in piano playing, had great instructors and a top-notch curriculum, and practiced your butt off for 15 hours, would you actually be any good at it? Not yet you wouldn't. You might be able to memorize your way through "When the Saints Go . . . Something, Something," but that'd be about the extent of your knowledge. But you *would* be good enough to continue learning more and practicing on your own. To become good at the piano, to be able to sit down and play any piece of music from a sheet, takes years. To be a master, and to sit down and play any piece of music beautifully, or by ear, can take a lifetime. Motorcycling is almost exactly the same.

While you won't be anything more than a bare beginner, you *will* walk away from the BRC with the three things new riders need most, whether you pass the class or not. First, you get your first 50 to 100 wobbly miles under your belt. This is the best gift you can give yourself, to work out those dangerous first kinks in a controlled environment, under the watchful eye of experienced coaches, and away from the perils of traffic and road hazards. Second, the BRC sends you off into the horizon with the tools (but not necessarily the *skills*) you need to begin practicing on your own, on the street, and in traffic. Both newbies and those who have, ahem, ridden on the street already, will be armed with the weapons of self-preservation—all they have to do is put them to use and practice, practice, practice. And last, the BRC is a ton of fun, and your first real experience as a motorcyclist in motion will be enjoyable and memorable and have you salivating for more.

The BRC uses drills designed to maximize your skill development in a very short period of time while allowing you to learn, practice, make mistakes, make leaps, and advance to the next level. But the BRC also relies heavily on your understanding that you're not "ready for anything" when it's all over. When you leave the course, you'll know exactly what your limitations are and what you need to do to improve. You'll also have the notes you made to yourself to help keep you focused.

What You'll Learn

Your time spent in the classroom will include learning about risk, preparation, the bike itself, basic and advanced riding skills, strategies for street riding, situations unique to motorcyclists, and the devastating effects of alcohol on riding skills. On the parking lot you'll get practice in the basic skills of starting and stopping, riding a controlled line, shifting, turning, and weaving. You'll also get practice in advanced skills like low-speed maneuvers and U-turns, higher-speed cornering and shifting, emergency braking, countersteering, and swerving. To pass the class, you'll need to demonstrate your knowledge on a written test and demonstrate your newfound skills on a riding test. Fortunately, you will have studied and practiced everything you need to know in the class, it will be fresh in your mind, and you'll have a dozen other people cheering you on as you do.

Now On to the Fun Stuff

Okay, you've completed your BRC and now it's time to get your wheels to the ground. Let the adventure begin! You may have gotten your license through the class or you may now be working up to taking the state riding test. Either way, you need to practice what you've learned to keep your skills fresh and sharp—and to improve.

You're going to approach street riding from the same perspective you approached your BRC. Armed with knowledge and the right tools, you're just going to jump in and learn how to ride by trial and error, experimentation, gradual phasing in of new techniques, and cementing them into your arsenal before moving on. The difference is now you have confidence that you did not have before, and now you have the freedom to try what you want, when you want, and practice as long as you want. Plus, you're probably seeing motorcycles in your sleep, and you're dying to get out there and turn some miles.

Too many riders get their training wheels off and expect that they're ready for anything the world can throw at them on the street. Smart riders know they need to ease into motorcycling, and never more so than at this stage of their development. It's a good idea at this time to practice in a particular way, a particular place, and with very particular goals in mind. Think back to Chapter 1. Remember Attitude Number 1? "Motorcyclists are responsible for everything that happens on the road." Here's your first chance to make that "fantasy" a reality. YOU control where and when you put yourself on the road, no one else does. Make the most of it. Now more than ever, it's imperative that you ride smart.

Armed with knowledge and the right tools, you're just going to jump in and learn how to ride by trial and error, experimentation, gradual phasing in of new techniques, and cementing them into your arsenal before moving on.

Be careful of putting yourself into complicated situations too early. When you first graduate the BRC, plan on spending some time away from traffic, on roads familiar to you, and with a definite plan in mind for what you're going to do, where you're going to do it, and why.

Improving Your Riding

Your goal is to start with what you know and ease into what you don't know gradually, taking small steps, and always having a familiar and comfortable place nearby to retreat and refocus. You're going to devise a practice plan that uses the skills you already have to develop the new skills you want and need. And you're going to time your practice sessions so you have very few distractions to deal with at first, but then adjust the when and the where that you practice to allow them into your plan one at a time. When you control how quickly new distractions come at you, you learn how to manage them without being instantly overwhelmed. You're going to be intelligent about the situations in which you place yourself and the goals you set in order to make maximum use of the skills you have *at that moment*.

Where to Go from Here

For now, stick to areas and roads you know like the back of your hand, and ride only during times of low traffic volume for the first week or two. Plan on staying close to your neighborhood—or at least a neighborhood that is intimately familiar to you—and venturing outside of that imaginary "boundary" only a block or two at a time as you grow accustomed to your bike.

Your first step is to devise a "training circuit." You can do it in your head, but you're way better off at this point to draw it out on a big sheet of paper, or the back of a big poster, or on a wall in your basement. Use big markers like you did way back in kindergarten and, literally, *draw* the roads that you're going to be practicing on. (You need to know these roads well enough to draw them from memory, dig?) You can even put big red X marks where you think you may have trouble. Draw arrows so you know which way you're going to go. Plan the whole damn thing out. This is the route you'll take every time you go out riding for the first 50–100 miles after graduating the BRC. The route should include left and right sharp turns, stop signs, left-hand and right-hand curves, and

hills. The farthest reaches of your route should never be more than a few miles from the safety of your driveway. Bear with me; it's just for the first week or two. Don't rush things now!

Plan this route carefully, study it, and memorize it. You should be able to sit in a chair, close your eyes, and follow the route in your mind, noting some landmarks along the way, seeing every turn and every stop, and knowing where any possible trouble areas are, like traffic or potholes.

Before every practice session, you're going to take a few minutes to sit on your bike and visualize the route you're about to take. This way, you'll see everything happen before you leave the driveway, so there won't be many surprises along the way. (This is a very advanced technique that experienced riders use all the time, and it will help you stay safe during those first critical miles, as well as for the rest of your riding career—use it!) What you're trying to avoid is Motorcyclist Information Overload. Whenever riders step outside of their comfort zone, they step into the realm of "too much, too soon." It's not guaranteed, but it's probable. By knowing what you'll encounter beforehand, that leaves a little more room in your brain for you to deal with what's new to you.

Your training circuit should be on low-speed roads of 25–35 miles per hour. Once you've completed and mastered all the basic skills on these roads, you'll deviate from the route to add short stints on unfamiliar or higher-speed roads (40, 45, 50 miles per hour) *a little at a time*, always reverting back to or finishing on your low-speed training circuit again. (Author's note: Visualize the Gary Larson *Far Side* cartoon in which a fish, holding his breath with his cheeks all puffed out, sneaks out of his "home pond" and runs to the pond on the other side of the road. The caption was "Great Moments in Evolution." THIS is what I'm talking about.) But don't add new roads willy-nilly. Think about them beforehand, plan them out, and memorize them.

Your first step is to devise a "training circuit." You can do it in your head, but you're way better off at this point to draw it out on a big sheet of paper, or the back of a big poster, or on a wall in your basement.

Ride only at low traffic volume times (weekday midmornings and weekend early mornings are best). As your confidence develops and experience grows, start to time your riding so it just barely overlaps with a busier time, such as weekend or weekday afternoons. You want to put yourself into the situation where you have an hour of good uncrowded practice—and five minutes of sheer metropolitan terror. When you can do five minutes without losing your cool, go for ten. When you can do ten, go for 20. Save the freeways, rush hour, and early evening riding for at least a month or 400 miles until you get comfortable sharing the road with other traffic.

An important warning: be careful not to put yourself into 55-mile-per-hour traffic before you're ready—you'll end up 10 miles per hour slower than the other traffic and paralyzed in your decision making. You'll lose focus, possibly surrender to fear, and probably get run over. Do not head out into high-speed traffic until you are willing to commit to riding at high speed! Work up to it gradually to build your confidence in yourself and your bike.

Do NOT, at this point in your evolution, ride at night or allow yourself to get caught out after dark. Even dusk is a bad time. Think: Soccer moms and hungry kids, cocktails and happy hour, and animals looking for food or romance. Don't venture out without all of your riding gear. If ever there was a time you'll need it, it's those first couple of weeks. And don't even THINK about carrying a passenger yet. (That's Chapter 7.)

Ride only at low traffic volume times (weekday midmornings and weekend early mornings are best). As your confidence develops and experience grows, start to time your riding so it just barely overlaps with a busier time, such as weekend or weekday afternoons.

Your first week or two riding should not be spontaneous, it should be carefully planned. Memorize your route beforehand so you can concentrate on developing your skills.

Think back to your BRC, take out your notes, and decide what your strengths and weaknesses are.

There are roads you know so well you could ride them in your sleep. For the first couple of weeks on your bike, stick to those roads and get intimately familiar with your bike before trying out any new tricks.

Don't Leave Anything up to Fate–You Decide

It's time for some more self-evaluation: Think back to your BRC, take out your notes, and decide what your strengths and weaknesses are. What skill did you struggle with the most? What skills came naturally for you? Which exercises were the most fun? In which exercises did you feel fear or anxiety? Why? What did the coaches have to say to you after the skill test? This is why it's so important to make good useful notes to yourself during the BRC. Use the answers to all these questions to fine-tune the following exercises into drills that maximize use of your strongest abilities and minimize the use of your weakest ones. Doing this will allow you to work on your weak points a little at a time, buttressed by the fun and confidence you get from riding to your strong points. Think of it as arm wrestling with your *good* arm.

Get Out and Get Some Exercise

Here are some basic practice drills to get you through your first few hundred miles after the BRC. Take them each individually at first, in whatever order you want, concentrating on only one at a time until it feels natural and requires very little mental effort. Then start combining them to two at a time. This will load down your mind and get you used to dealing with multiple priorities—but they're still priorities that *you* choose. (During normal street riding, priorities will choose *you*, so get familiar with juggling riding factors in your own time, at your own pace, to build your mental ability to absorb it when you have to.) Keep combining different exercises until you feel you can handle everything at once. When that time comes, you're ready to move on to Chapter 5. Mastering these exercises should take you two weeks to a month, more than that if you don't have three or four nights to ride every week.

Exercise 1: Stopping on a Dime
Pick out stopping points and work at bringing your bike to a smooth stop with the contact patch of your front tire exactly where you want it to be. Do this from different speeds: 10, 20, and 30 miles per hour. This will give you skill in estimating your stopping distance and modulating your brakes to time your braking perfectly. Keep your head up and eyes on the horizon for better balance. Don't jump into quick stops just yet; the stops you're practicing here are planned stops, just like you'll do every time you ride.

Contact Patch: The part of a motorcycle's tires that comes into contact with the ground.

Take them each individually at first, in whatever order you want, concentrating on only one at a time until it feels natural and requires very little mental effort.

Your goal is to develop a "feel" for shifting based on the situation or how the bike sounds, so you can shift in the real world without having to consciously work through the steps.

Exercise 2:
Turning Sharply
Focus on your finishing line when making slow, tight turns. Arbitrarily pick out a lane position (left third, middle third, right third, just off the centerline, or just off the fogline) and practice turning your bike from the old path of travel to the new one in one smooth arc. Decide on your line before you turn, then keep your head and eyes looking well through the turn the whole time. Use your peripheral vision to gauge how close you are to your line.

Keep practicing this exercise until you can find the line you want every time without having to make mid- or late-corner steering adjustments and without staring at the ground in front of you. This takes a while to perfect, so don't get down on yourself if it takes a while to master. In the real world, you'll have to adjust your line for traffic and surface hazards like gravel or oil in advance, and doing this on purpose without these hazards is a great way to build this skill.

Finishing Line: The motorcycle's path of travel relative to the dividing lines (centerline and fogline, yellow and white, respectively) after completing a corner.

Peripheral Vision: The area of a rider's vision that is *not* in the crosshairs. Example: Staring at the rear window (crosshairs) of a vehicle directly in front of you, the centerline, fogline, oncoming traffic, and road signs are in your peripheral vision.

Exercise 3: Shifting without Thinking
Spend time focusing solely on shifting. In particular, get to know which gear feels best at what speed, which gear you use for cornering, and how you time your downshifting when coming to a stop or slowing for a corner. Work on shifting more quickly and efficiently, using both hands simultaneously. Your goal is to develop a "feel" for shifting based on the situation or how the bike sounds, so you can shift in the real world without having to consciously work through the steps. This will require a lot—perhaps years—of practice to really get it right. Don't sweat it. Even the best riders could probably use more practice and instruction on their shifting.

Exercise 4: Cornering with Confidence

You're going to find some faster curves posted at 30–35 miles per hour and approach them aggressively to really learn to countersteer the bike. Take your bike up to the speed limit, keep it there as you approach the curve, and hold that speed for as long as you feel comfortable. Then roll off the throttle, brake if necessary, and set an entry speed of 20–25 miles per hour. Remember to use the outside-inside-outside (see diagram in Chapter 3) path of travel, unless oncoming traffic dictates you have to stay away from the centerline. Once you've set your entry speed, start rolling gently on the throttle to settle the bike. Then look through the turn, press on the handlebar to initiate the lean, and continue rolling on the throttle all the way through the turn, wicking the bike back up to the speed limit.

Exercise 5: Emergency Braking

On your circuit, every once in a while, when there is no traffic behind you, bring your bike to a sudden emergency stop. Imagine a car pulled out in front of you, or a little kid ran out from behind some bushes, or you missed the yellow and the light suddenly turned red on you. Do this from several different speeds to learn brake modulation in different situations. Your goal is to bring the bike to a safe stop as quickly as you possibly can.

Stopping quickly is fairly straightforward, but combining downshifting with an emergency stop takes quite a bit of practice. For your first few stops, focus more on the downshifting to get a feel for both hands and both feet working at once. When you have the basic motions down, start braking harder, stopping the bike quicker. Your head and eyes should be up and focused on the horizon for balance and control.

Front Brake Advice: Use it as if you're trying to squeeze the juice out of an orange. One firm, progressive squeeze, lightly at first, then harder and harder and harder until the bike comes to a complete stop. If the front wheel locks up, immediately release the front brake and reapply it, remembering to squeeze it progressively and not "grab" the brake.

Rear Brake Advice: You'll find as you get better and better at emergency stops that the rear brake will have a tendency to lock up. As you improve, work at releasing a little pressure from the rear brake as you increase pressure on the front. If the rear wheel locks up, it's smartest at this point to keep it locked until you're completely stopped by keeping pressure on the rear brake. If your head and eyes are focused where they should be (on the horizon) and you're not on a weird slope, the bike should skid in a mostly straight line with the rear wheel locked. Not that you'd want to get too used to this, but it helps to have a handle on the feeling if you ever need to use it on a slippery surface or in gravel.

Stopping quickly is fairly straightforward, but combining downshifting with an emergency stop takes quite a bit of practice.

Even under hard braking, with the forks compressed and the rear wheel inching skyward, your visual focus should be two to four seconds ahead.

This photo is by John Gateley. And yes, ladies, he's single too.

Stability Problems: If you find that you're almost going to fall over every time you do an emergency stop, it's because your handlebars are not square when you finally come to a halt. To practice overcoming this, brake hard down to about 5 miles per hour or so, then ease off the brakes ever so slightly and square the handlebars as you're just about to stop. This will help you stop smoothly and safely. As you get better at it, brake hard down to 4 miles per hour, then 3 miles per hour, and so on. In the real world, you'll rarely need to come to a *complete* stop in an emergency—and sometimes it's not advisable to do so. This will help you learn to scrub off a lot of speed but still be in control of a moving, stable motorcycle when the drama's over, so you can be on your way again.

Exercise 6: Smooth It Out

Once you have stopping, turning, shifting, and cornering in your riding arsenal and you can do them without too much conscious thought, it's time to start making it *look* good. You're going to set a goal to be as smooth as glass in everything you do. A well-controlled motorcycle in motion is a beautiful thing to see. Work on riding as *fluidly* as you possibly can. You're shooting to make an observer unaware that you're doing anything at all: from riding to braking without a bob of the headlight, from braking to turning without a wobble of the taillight, from turning to accelerating (and smoothly disappearing from view!) without compressing the rear end or honking a telltale exhaust note.

Becoming a smooth rider is a lifelong task, and not easy to master—enjoy the challenge and have fun with it. You will absolutely never, ever, be able to ride so smoothly that you couldn't ride smoother; a real enthusiast will never, ever, be able to ride as smoothly as he or she really wants. With time, the smoothness will come and your riding will look as good as an eagle in flight or a shark in the water. If that's too predatory an analogy, a smooth rider will look like an otter having a blast in the river. Oh, wait—they're predators, too.

Becoming a smooth rider is a lifelong task, and not easy to master— enjoy the challenge and have fun with it.

Exercise 7: Swerving around (Imaginary) Obstacles

Making quick direction or path of travel changes is critical to avoiding hazards. When traffic allows, pick imaginary points (or real ones, like a manhole cover, pothole, etc.) and swerve around them. Remember, swerving is just quick countersteering, first right, then left, or vice versa. Let the bike lean and turn underneath you while you keep your body upright and loose, head and eyes focused on your escape route. Be careful to keep your throttle steady and never use your brakes while swerving. Your goal is to steer quickly, abandon one path of travel and find another, and then continue on your way.

Remember, swerving is just quick countersteering, first right, then left, or vice versa.

What People Say and What People Mean Number 4: "What Do Little Cones and Painted Lines Have to Do with Motorcycling?"

There are two types of riders in the world: Those who "get it" and those who don't. The Hindu tradition suggests that those who say the least are the ones who are truly wise, and those who say a lot really don't know what they're talking about. (If they understood, they'd shut up . . . get it?) While this may not always be 100 percent true, when it comes to motorcycling, there's merit there.

Lots of whiners complain about the state skill test. "The test is too *hard* on a big bike." "Why would I ever ride at 20 miles per hour toward a *brick wall*?" And the best one, "What does riding around *little cones* and *painted lines* have to do with motorcycling?" These are people who just don't get it. And they're showing you just how badly they don't get it by opening their mouths when they should be thinking hard about what they might be missing. Ignorance makes a lot of noise, while wisdom rides off into the sunset, quietly going about the business of knowing stuff.

The test is not unfair for riders with big bikes; big bikes simply require more skill to ride than small ones. If those riders on their great big bikes can't pass the test, those great big bikes are probably too much for them to handle in the real world, too. They should either get a smaller bike (what are all those cubic inches compensating for, anyway?) or learn how to ride the big one. Either way, tell them to quit *whining*. They're not being persecuted, they just chose a bike that requires a little more skill to ride. The morons who take the test on little borrowed bikes, then hop on their 1,400-cc Intimidacruisers, are fooling no one but themselves. You have to build up to a bike like that.

Further, while the real-world relevance of riding around little cones and lines may be debatable, the skills that the exercises measure are not. Low-speed balance and control, turning, stopping, and swerving are skills critical to your survival on a motorcycle. Think back a few pages. Remember how it's easier to ride a bike fast than it is to ride a bike slowly? Doing these things correctly at 10 or 15 miles per hour shows that you're capable of doing them at 40 or 60— and it doesn't work the other way around. To those whiners who think the test is useless, I say quit showing everyone how ignorant you are about motorcycling and accept the fact that you have more to learn.

Doing these things correctly at 10 or 15 miles per hour shows that you're capable of doing them at 40 or 60—and it doesn't work the other way around.

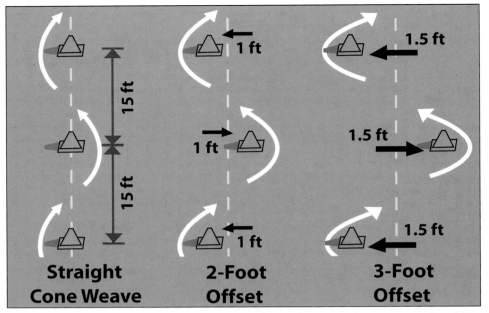

| Straight Cone Weave | 2-Foot Offset | 3-Foot Offset |

Start with the cones all in a line and about ten to fifteen feet apart. As you get comfortable with the weave, start moving the cones outward, the first cone to the left, the next to the right, and so on. Eventually, you'll want to have the cones offset two to three feet.

When you finally do get your motorcycle endorsement, whether from taking the test or taking the BRC, don't dupe yourself into thinking you've learned everything you need to know to be a good rider.

Exercise 8: Cone Weave and U-Turns
This is all great fun riding around and practicing, but you'll still need to be sharp on your low-speed maneuvers. Any monkey can ride a bike at 30 miles per hour on big wide streets and not have too much trouble changing direction. But what about tight spaces, like driveways or crowded parking lots? Find a quiet place off-street with lots of room, set up a cone weave, and start practicing. Being able to putz your bike through an offset cone weave is a real show of skill. To add variety, take breaks from cone weaves and work on your U-turns. Start with a U-turn area 30 feet wide, and work your way down to 20 feet.

> **Escape Route:** A *preplanned* path of travel a rider uses in an emergency.

For both cone weaves and U-turns, clutch and throttle control make all the difference. You'll need to be very, very smooth. Try them in both first and second gear and see which one you like better. Many times it may be smoother to use your clutch to control your speed and keep your throttle constant or at idle. Keep your head and eyes up and focused on where you want your bike to be, not at the cones.

Licensed for Action
After all this training and practicing, you're about ready to take the test to get your license. Some vehicles, like big trucks and school buses, require a special license to drive. Because motorcycles require special knowledge and skills, they require a special endorsement as well. If you took a BRC, chances are you got your motorcycle endorsement that way, but that's not always the case.

Don't underestimate what a motorcycle endorsement means. You may think you know how to operate your bike, but until you can pass a test demonstrating that, you may not be quite as good as you think. A lot of people (who fail the skill test time and time again) believe the test for a motorcycle license is too difficult; most experienced riders agree that it's actually far too *easy*. If you're having trouble passing the test, it doesn't mean you're not allowed to ride, it just means you're not ready for your license yet.

Most states start you on an instruction permit, which is a temporary license so

Congratulations! You've successfully learned how to ride and earned your motorcycle license. It took a lot of hard work to get to this point, but don't rest on your laurels just yet. You have years of learning, experience, and growth before you are a true motorcyclist. The journey has only just begun.

Any monkey can ride a bike at 30 miles per hour on big wide streets and not have too much trouble changing direction.

you can practice on the street. Passing the permit test shows you have at least a basic understanding of what motorcycling is all about. However, permits usually also have restrictions that a full motorcycle license doesn't, such as daytime-only, maximum speed limits, no freeways, no passengers, and mandatory protective gear (usually just a helmet). These are all factors that, if taken lightly, can pose inordinate risks to new motorcyclists. Once you're good enough to pass the skill test and get your full license, then you can take these things on, but while you're learning, it's best to remove those variables from the picture whether your license says you can or not.

When you finally do get your motorcycle endorsement, whether from taking the test or taking the BRC, don't dupe yourself into thinking you've learned everything you need to know to be a good rider. You haven't. You've learned the *bare minimum* you need to know to ride on public roads. Once you're legal to ride without restrictions, life as a motorcyclist officially begins. Now you can get out there and have some fun, learn new tricks and deepen your knowledge and skill, and really start to learn what true motorcycling is all about. You're about to head deeper into the water to see just how far down this iceberg goes.

Recommended Reading:
Internet new-rider forums—a Google search for "motorcycle forums" will turn up hundreds of sites on which new and experienced riders share information. Read up, ask questions, and learn from others' experiences.

www.motorcyclesafety.org—go to "Safety Tips" and take a look at information about braking, cornering, riding strategy, carrying passengers, etc. Great riding tips developed by the author and several volunteer expert motorcyclists.

GETTING FAMILIAR

Y BUYING YOUR BIKE AND RIDING GEAR, TAKING THE BRC, PRACTICING YOUR SKILLS, AND TAKING THE TEST AND GETTING YOUR LICENSE, YOU'VE OFFICIALLY STEPPED INTO THE WORLD OF MOTORCYCLING—A SECRET WORLD THAT ONLY ABOUT 1 IN 10 PEOPLE EVER EXPERIENCE.

You've joined an elite group that knows the joy and satisfaction that two-wheeled travel brings to the table. And you've done it the smart way, through knowledge and training and preparation, understanding all the time that there are things about motorcycling that you just don't understand.

It's critical to keep that attitude for just a while longer. I know you want to get out there and ride the wheels off that thing, but hold on. Not just yet.

While it seems easy to take the class and get your license and just get out there and do it, you're still just a beginner and need to take the next steps very carefully with a strong understanding of your limitations. How many hours of practice do you have? Twenty? Thirty? Right now all you know how to do is operate the bike. It's going to take some serious and planned effort to learn how to *ride*. It's going to take even more to learn how to *use* the bike. What I'm saying is: Don't dive in headfirst. Not yet. There are still a few things you need to know.

Now that you're a full-fledged motorcyclist, you've got a lot of decisions to make. While you're probably jazzed that you passed your test and are now legal to ride on the street, you're not even close to being ready yet. Take your time, use your head, and work up to street riding gradually.

Humans learn, not by being told, but by pushing up against their boundaries and either being successful or getting rebuffed. Motorcyclists learn the same way. Nudge up against your boundaries, but don't take the chainsaw to 'em just yet.

What you'll get from this book that you won't find anywhere else is a plan to get you from eager 100-mile novice to comfortable 5,000-mile rider. The exercises in the last chapter got you comfortable riding on the street. In this chapter you'll get some good advice on making the leap into traffic while keeping yourself and your environment under your control. There are good and bad ways to learn the ropes—knowing your skill level and boundaries, and pushing out along those boundaries little by little is the smartest way. I'm going to teach you how to do it.

Big Secret Number 5: Automatic Motorcycling

Learning to ride a motorcycle is like learning to tie your shoes when you were a little kid. The first few times the process was bewildering. Someone was coaching you through it, you somehow managed to get from Point A to Point B, but you didn't really remember exactly how you got there. You probably talked yourself through it—over, under, in, and out—and it was frustrating and took a lot longer than it should have. You probably tied really horrible knots and needed a lot of help along the way.

But something magical happened over time: you started getting better at it. You learned to do it right—maybe not great, but *correctly*—every time. You got quicker. You eventually learned to tie nice, square knots, and you did it without really thinking about it and without any outside help. Your hands knew the trick and did their thing on their own, and it required less concentration. Now you can tie your shoes while you talk on the phone or watch TV. Because your body memorized the motions, your mind became free to do other things.

The same thing happens with motorcycling. While your body is learning to work the bike, it requires all of your concentration. It can be frustrating, and you don't always do it very well. But as your hands and feet get familiar with the controls, you think about them less and less and your mind is freed up and ready to start learning again. Now it's time to start packing in more information, because you've got the room for it—and you need it.

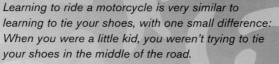

Learning to ride a motorcycle is very similar to learning to tie your shoes, with one small difference: When you were a little kid, you weren't trying to tie your shoes in the middle of the road.

There are good and bad ways to learn the ropes— knowing your skill level and boundaries, and pushing out along those boundaries little by little is the smartest way.

Important note: When you want to explore your limits and push out at your boundaries, it's absolutely critical that you clear everything else from your mind and concentrate on riding. When you get a little better at riding and you have more experience, you don't need to work so hard to clear your mind, but for now, take that extra 60 seconds or so to focus.

As you practice, gain experience, and learn, your limitations become fewer and fewer.

Proficiency on a Scale of 1 to 10

Riding a motorcycle is all about knowing, and remaining within, your limitations. This means always riding with something "in reserve." Your reserve is extra attention, time and space to maneuver, and escape routes—plans B and C in case plan A isn't going over so well. This also means avoiding riding right up against the limits of your mind, your body, your bike, and your environment. As you practice, gain experience, and learn, your limitations become fewer and fewer. You will still ride with a reserve; it's just that your reserve won't need to be as great as when you were a newbie.

Let's hypothetically place your riding ability on a scale of 1 to 10. "One" represents the most ability: A veteran rider with a safety-conscious attitude, loads of training, expert motorcycle skills, superior defensive riding strategies, and a lifetime of experience and knowledge. On the other end of the spectrum, "ten" represents the least ability: a complete tenderfoot who has never ridden a motorcycle—in fact, one who can't tell his motorcycle from his elbow stuck in a hole in the ground.

On this scale, let's pretend this newbie rider at level 10 has a 100 percent chance of getting in over his or her head. That makes sense. If you have no experience or training or even any knowledge of

motorcycling, you're pretty much in over your head as soon as you turn the key. An expert rider at level 1, however, has only a 10 percent chance of getting in over his or her head. That makes sense, too: it *could* happen, but with all that training, tons of knowledge, and 20 years' experience, you're going to make all the right decisions 9 times out of 10. Comparing the two, the expert rider at level 1 is probably 10 times better than the newbie rider at level 10.*

(*That's being *generous*. If you're at all mathematically inclined, the most realistic scale would actually be a logarithm where every level means half the chance and twice the skill as a rider at the next level, but that would be just a little too elaborate for what we're trying to accomplish here. If you want to argue the point, direct it to ridesmart@gmail.com, but I'll warn you, I tried, and there was just no good way to explain it without finger puppets and funny voices.)

These are not meant to be real numbers, they're meant to help you evaluate your *relative* ability with guidelines and checkpoints along the way. Just because you're at level 10 doesn't mean you have a 100 percent chance of crashing; it only means you are that much more likely than a level 9 rider, or a level 2 rider, to crash. If you're a weak rider, you could have 20 years of experience and have done everything possible to learn about motorcycling, but still be riding at a level 5 simply because that's who you are. A strong rider could have only two years of experience, but because of natural ability, vast knowledge, and additional training, could be riding at a level 3. You have to be honest with yourself and be careful not to overestimate your abilities.

You're also going to need to be keenly aware of how riding ability changes from day to day based on your body, your mind, your emotions, and your activities. Some days you may feel like a million bucks. Other days you may feel that your brain is running on only one cylinder (sorry, single-thumper bike owners!). If you're distracted, pissed off, hungry, or tired, you may not be able to ride normally—take yourself down a notch on the riding ability scale, realize that you're that much more likely to get in over your head, and adjust your riding accordingly by giving yourself more reserve. On the other hand, if you had a good night's rest and no distractions or emotions clogging up your concentration, you may be able to ride better than normal, and you can crank it up a notch, experiment, and push a little at the boundaries of your reserve because your mind and body are 100 percent *there*.

Level / Title		BRC*	Experience	Additional Knowledge
1	Expert	Yes	20 Years	All**
2	Expert	Yes	10 Years	All**
3	Rider	Yes	5 Years	Much (Adv. Training)
4	Rider	Yes	4 Years	Much (Adv. Training)
5	Rookie	Yes	3 Years	Some (Books)
6	Rookie	Yes	2 Years	Some (Books)
7	Novice	Yes	1.5 Years	Minimal (Magazines)
8	Novice	Yes	1 Year	Minimal (Magazines)
9	Newbie	Yes	6 Months	None
10	Newbie	No	None	None

*Any rider who hasn't taken a BRC (see Chapter 4) automatically moves down one level.
** "All" represents a rider doing everything he or she possibly can to improve his or her riding: reading magazines, books, taking advanced training, studying research reports and statistics, participating in track days or racing, teaching the BRC, etc. These are not meant to be real numbers; they're meant to help you evaluate your relative ability with guidelines and checkpoints along the way. Just because you're at level 10 doesn't mean you have a 100 percent chance of crashing; it only means you are that much more likely than a level 9 rider, or a level 2 rider, to crash. Weak riders could have 20 years of experience and have done everything possible to learn about motorcycling, but still be riding at a level 5 simply because that's who they are. A strong rider could have only two years of experience, but because of natural ability, vast knowledge, and additional training, could be riding at a level 3. You have to be honest with yourself and careful not to overestimate your abilities.

If you're distracted, pissed off, hungry, or tired, you may not be able to ride normally—take yourself down a notch on the riding ability scale, realize that you're that much more likely to get in over your head, and adjust your riding accordingly by giving yourself more reserve.

Experience	Minutes/Ride
BRC	20
Week 1	20
Week 2	30
Week 3	40
Week 4	50
Week 5	60
Week 6	70
Week 7	80
Week 8	90

Adding ten minutes to your normal ride after the first week increases your exposure to riding 50 percent! Adding ten minutes after your second month only increases it about 10 percent. Be careful not to bite off too much too soon during your first month. You have to learn to walk before you can run.

For your first few street adventures, keep your riding to short intervals, 30 to 40 minutes tops, and gradually add minutes every time you go out.

Go with What You Know

Like the training circuit you used to practice after the BRC, stick close to what you know for the first few months. When the roads or roadway types are familiar to you, that's one less thing you have to think about so you'll be more ready for surprises. Keep to the areas with which you are familiar and the neighborhoods you recognize. If you're used to driving in the suburbs, stay in the suburbs. If you're used to driving at city speeds (30–40 miles per hour) and not freeway speeds (55–70 miles per hour), stick to the roads with the lower speed limits. When you go out riding, plan your route ahead of time to help you stay within your comfort zone. At this point in your riding career, every little edge you can give yourself is critical.

Bite-Size Steps

Another way to stick with what you know is to keep your ride length and riding time consistent. Work up to longer rides gradually. While you're learning, your mind and your body will become fatigued more easily than when you have some experience. When you start to droop, your skills and your attention suffer, and you don't want to put yourself into a bad situation without realizing it. In the BRC, you were riding exercises that lasted for about 20 minutes. When you were practicing on your training circuit, you probably only rode for 20 to 40 minutes at a stretch. That's still twice as long as you'd ridden before! Now is not the time to overestimate your abilities and head out for a two-hour ride. For your first few street adventures, keep your riding to short intervals, 30 to 40 minutes tops, and gradually add minutes every time you go out. Don't jump more than about 10 minutes per week. Within a couple of months, you'll be used to longer rides of an hour or more, and adding time to those rides won't be so dramatic to your brain and your body.

Mental Overload

I want you to try this, even if only mentally: Go to a supermarket. Walk

During the first couple months, don't bite off more riding than you're used to chewing. If you get caught in bad weather, feel overly tired, or overwhelmed, you don't want to be too far from home.

If you build up your riding a little at a time, your mind will learn and adapt as you go.

down one aisle at your regular walking pace and try to memorize as many of the products on the shelves as you can. When you get to the end of the aisle, write them all down on a pad of paper, and count how many you remembered. Now go to the next aisle. You're going to do the same thing, except this time you're going to run down the aisle as fast as you can. How many products could you memorize this time?

When you venture into higher speeds and unfamiliar territory, your mind will not be as efficient scanning for hazards and reacting to changes as it is at lower speeds and in places you know like the back of your hand. If you build up your riding a little at a time, your mind will learn and adapt as you go. However, if you take on too much too early in your riding experience, you'll find yourself in a state of mental overload. In traffic, this can be fatal. Because you're new and trying to learn, this is bound to happen to you. Pay attention to the warning signs and know how to deal with it when it comes.

Problem Mental overload: too much coming at you too fast.

Solution 1 Slow down to separate hazards in time and space.
Solution 2 Change route to a slower one with fewer hazards.
Solution 3 Pull off the road and take a break. Refocus.
Solution 4 Park and wait a few hours for traffic to die down.
Solution 5 Quit for the day. Have someone pick you up.

The first time the jack-in-the-box pops out at you, you're surprised. The second time, you're a little more ready for it. You're still surprised, but not nearly as much as the first time. This is what visualizing potential hazards can do for you.

The best way to recover from mental overload is to reduce your speed if you can.

When things start coming at you faster than your mind can sort them out, it's time to slow down, pull over, or quit for the day. For example, any time you're surprised by anyone or anything on the road, such as a cat driving a car that suddenly changes lanes on you (cats aren't very good drivers) or a pothole filled with pointy screwdrivers that leaves you no time to react, *more than once every few minutes*, you're in mental overload and you need to dial it back a click. I emphasize *more than once* because surprises happen all the time. Lots of people make mistakes on the road (including riders) and this is to be expected. But, when these surprises begin to "pile up" on you, it's no longer the surprises that are the problem, it's you.

The best way to recover from mental overload is to reduce your speed if you can. Wind it down enough (it usually only takes a 5- or 10-mile-per-hour reduction) that you don't have to deal with more

than one thing at a time. Just like walking instead of running down the supermarket aisle, the slower speed will allow your mind to keep up with the road. However, most traffic doesn't deal well with a rolling roadblock, and a slow-moving motorcycle is a target—might as well paint a great big red-and-white bull's-eye on your back! If that's the case, it may be better to find a different route, one that moves slower and has fewer surprises, or at least the surprises are separated a little better in time and space. (This is why it's important to go with what you know, and pick your route carefully.)

If neither option is reasonable, you need to get out of that situation and collect yourself. Safely turn off the road or into a parking lot, shut down the bike, and relax. Revisualize the route ahead of you, all the turns and stops and curves you'll need to take to get home, and memorize it again so you don't have to think about it as much while you're moving. Also, visualize the types of surprises you're likely to see between where you are and home. Imagination can take a lot of the drama out of road hazards. When some yutz tosses a half-eaten sandwich out the car window at you, it won't distract you as much, because you've seen that before.

If you get back out onto the road and you're immediately overwhelmed again, you've gone beyond your limits for the day. Get off the road and wait for the traffic to die down, or call someone to come and pick you up. Don't force yourself to ride in situations in which you are not comfortable. Live to fight another day.

Focus on Your Strong Suits

Excellence doesn't come from avoiding bad habits. Excellence comes from indulging good habits. During this time of skill development you need to play up your good skills and play down your weaker skills. By that I mean stick to your strengths and, little by little, your weaknesses will fall into line and improve along with the rest of you. Stick to the roads and the type of riding you're good at, the ones that make you feel confident and skilled. Avoid plunging into tricky areas and instead deal with them in small bites.

You've spent a lot of time at a "low level" of motorcycle involvement with restrictions on when and where you ride, some imposed by your learner's permit, some imposed by your own sense of self-preservation. Stick with those limitations: Don't ride at night, wear all your riding gear, stay off the freeways, and don't carry a passenger. It's also a good idea to not combine riding with any other activity like work, play, or running errands. Those little distractions can cause you big trouble. And no matter how much you want to, you're not yet ready to ride with others or in a group. We'll get to these things in the next two chapters.

Avoid plunging into tricky areas and instead deal with them in small bites.

Group riding is a whole new can of worms. Don't be tempted to try it until you have at least six months of riding under your belt. We'll get to group riding in Chapter 7. Dean Groover courtesy *Motorcycle Cruiser*.

What People Say and
What People Mean Number 5:
"Laying It Down"

"I was out ridin' and this car pulls out in front of me. I had to lay 'er down."

I have heard this statement many times, and I can't think of a more moronic thing for a motorcyclist to say. What people mean when they say this is "I don't know how to control my bike, and I'm an idiot, so I locked up the rear brake and crashed on purpose."

But, what they *really* mean is: "This car pulls out in front of me. I had no warning, no time, and no room to stop. And since I don't know how to use my brakes, I accidentally locked them up and crashed. And because it was someone else's fault, I refuse to take responsibility for it, so I'm going to pretend that I did it on purpose so no one knows what a moron I am." The rider could use a nice frosty can of Attitude Number 1 and realize that he or she is responsible for other drivers' actions as well as his or her own.

These people are fooling themselves. They do not—and probably never will—understand that they need to learn something more about riding. They'll spend the rest of their life blaming some dumb driver for forcing them to crash.

A smart rider understands that people *will* pull out in front of motorcycles all the time. (In fact, a smart rider is way beyond that—remember Attitude Number 2? You are expecting that everyone else on the road is deliberately trying to kill you. This mindset sets you up to assume that people will pull out in front of you!) An intelligent rider positions the bike carefully in traffic and draws attention with brightly colored protective gear. And a smart rider spent 15 hours in the BRC and learned how to use the brakes properly, and can get the bike stopped quickly *without* laying it on the ground. Riders who have never taken the BRC tend to be afraid of the front brake and overuse the rear brake, which can easily lead to a crash.

Crashing on purpose is NOT an option to any semi-intelligent rider. The bike will stop a lot quicker with its rubber on the ground, rather than sliding along on its side. If you don't know how to use your brakes there's an easy solution: learn. But *don't* fall into the trap of blaming another motorist when your skills—if you had learned and practiced them—could have prevented a crash.

"This car pulls out in front of me. I had no warning, no time, and no room to stop."

Many times when someone "lays it down" they never even hit the car they were trying to avoid. Riders who knew how to use their brakes could have stopped the bike without crashing and continued on their way. This rider has made a bad decision, but will forever be blaming someone else for the mistake.

Making the Leaps

Before too long you're going to feel like you're ready for anything. That's good. Now is the time you're also going to start climbing up a new learning curve. This leap up the motorcyclist food chain is a big jump. You'll be about to the point that you don't really have to think very hard about operating the bike, and instead you'll begin to think about strategy—how to ride the bike in different types of traffic and on a variety of roadway designs. You get to be a beginning motorcyclist all over again.

Riding environments fall into four basic types: rural roads and highways, multilane freeways, suburban arterials, and city surface streets. Each one has its place in the hierarchy of risk and each one has its unique hazards. We're going to look at these situations from a big-picture perspective to give you a good understanding of what you're getting into.

As mentioned in Chapter 1, the road is a system designed solely for getting from point A to point B. Ideally, every road would go straight to the place you want it to go, with no natural or man-made obstructions along the way. (Well, that's no longer entirely true. Now you're a motorcyclist, so the ideal road would include a nearly endless series of challenging and gravel-free curves, but let's not go off into la-la land just yet.) Unfortunately it doesn't work like that, but a smart rider can use general principles to guide his or her riding strategy.

Riding environments fall into four basic types: rural roads and highways, multilane freeways, suburban arterials, and city surface streets.

How you break the ice with high-risk situations like city driving, country road corner-carving, and freeway commuting can build your skills or it can destroy your confidence. Know what you're getting into before you head out.

Rule 1: As speed increases, risk increases.

Sure, you look at these signs and they tell you how fast you're allowed to go, but when you look at these signs, do they tell you something about what to expect? They should.

The Speed/Predictability Relationship

The two easiest survival concepts a rider can learn are those associated with speed and traffic predictability. Speed and risk have a parallel relationship. As speed increases, so does a rider's risk. Hazards approach the rider at a faster rate and the consequences of a crash are likely to be greater. A rider on a stationary bike in the garage faces almost no risk at all of a mishap. But as that rider moves away from 0 miles per hour and out into the great blue yonder, his or her risk goes up. At 30 miles per hour a rider faces a great deal more risk than at 0 miles per hour; a rider at 60 miles per hour faces a great deal more than at 30, and so on. Therefore, a high-speed road is more risky than a low-speed road, all else being equal.

Rule 1: As speed increases, risk increases.

At the same time, predictability and risk have an opposite relationship. As traffic predictability decreases, a rider's risk increases. Some roads and some types of traffic are more predictable than others; a rider's absolute best defense on the road is being a good "predictor" of what other drivers will do. The more surprises a road throws at you, the higher the risk. For example, a road with lots of intersecting traffic and a variety of speeds, such as a city street, is a lot less predictable than a road with little inter-secting traffic and similar speeds, like a freeway. Therefore, a road with lots of intersections is more risky than one with few intersections.

Rule 2: As predictability decreases, risk increases.

So the safest motorcycle roads would be those that combine low speed and high predictability, right? The problem is that there are no such roads. This is the speed/predictability conundrum, and it's a stormy relationship. Due to the way roads are designed, as speed increases (risk goes up), predictability also increases (risk goes down); as speed decreases (risk goes down), predictability also decreases (risk goes up). So in either case the overall amount of risk doesn't change much; what changes are the *types* of risk you face.

The long and short is that the less predictable the road, the more likely you are to be surprised and involved in a crash . . . but the less likely you are to be hurt, because you're not riding so fast. The faster the road, the less likely you are to be surprised and involved in a crash—because the road's more predictable—but the more likely you are to get hurt if you do crash because of the higher speed. See the problem?

Rule 3: On slower roads, you have more chance of crashing but less chance of dying; on faster roads, you have less chance of crashing but more chance of dying.*

* *Exception*: Rural roads combine the unpredictability and varied speeds of city streets and residential neighborhoods with the high speeds of freeways—and almost always represent the majority of fatal motorcycle crashes. Murphy's Law strikes again: the best places to ride are also the most dangerous!

Rule 2: As predictability decreases, risk increases.

Rule 3: On slower roads, you have more chance of crashing but less chance of dying; on faster roads, you have less chance of crashing but more chance of dying.*

City Streets and Residential Neighborhoods

With city streets, what you have are roads that are too small for the number of vehicles they carry. The distractions and traffic they present are too unpredictable for anything more than about 20 miles per hour. (This applies primarily to city streets.) *These streets were never meant to be streets.* They began life oh-so-long-ago as the narrow gaps between two buildings, the dividing lines between two pieces of property, or the empty space between two neighborhoods. They're not necessarily dangerous, but consider anything more than walking speed "red-alert speed."

Neighborhood roads are too small and offer too many distractions, but what compounds the risk is that they're adjacent to 45-mile-per-hour arterials and 65-mile-per-hour freeways. That's not so different from the city, except instead of grownups going to work, going shopping, or heading off somewhere to explore, you have kids walking home from school, getting off the bus, or carelessly chasing each other in their own neighborhoody way. In residential areas, 30 miles per hour may seem S-L-O-W to someone coming right off the freeway after a hard day of work, but if you're a mother with three kids playing Frisbee in the street, even 20 seems too fast.

Roads that go through cities or neighborhoods are confusing at best, but regular. The stop signs and stoplights occur every couple of blocks or so. The cars parked along the curb regularly dart out or open doors into traffic. Pedestrians regularly run across the street to catch the bus. The other drivers that travel city streets are either too familiar with them or completely lost: expect other drivers to be lazy or clueless.

Neighborhood roads are too small and offer too many distractions, but what compounds the risk is that they're adjacent to 45-mile-per-hour arterials and 65-mile-per-hour freeways.

The only thing predictable about low-speed surface streets is their unpredictability. Expect the worst to happen all the time and you'll be pleasantly surprised. Expect everyone to behave predictably and you'll be surprised time and time again—and not in a good way.

Suburban Streets and Exurban Roads

Here you have people used to having a lot of space and a big, safe car with which to get around in it. These roads were once smaller roads that evolved with the surrounding communities and were forced to get bigger along with population growth. Stoplights here come only once every half-mile or so; the yellow (or red) light at said stoplights is unfortunately considered an advisory and not a rule. Plan on dealing with drivers distracted by work, home, whatever errand they're running at the moment, or just by the fact that they know the roads and the timing of the lights and are flying on autopilot to wherever they're going.

Expect people in the suburbs to be bored with driving and merely going through the motions of operating a two- or three-ton vehicle amidst the rest of the world.

Freeways and Multilane Highways

These are (theoretically) carefully planned, high-speed routes designed so motorists can cover a large distance in a short amount of time. This means jumping onto the highway means jumping into a *machine.*

This machine is designed to move traffic. It's a conveyor belt. Speeds are regulated, exits and entrances are controlled, and distractions are few. So what you get is a complete system of brain-dead road users, tooling along in whichever lane seems like the best idea at the time, never really opening their eyes until their EXIT NOW sign appears on the horizon. They generally don't make any sudden or unusual moves—but when they do, when someone does something *way* out of the ordinary, get yourself the hell away from there. At 65 miles per hour with 10,000 other users on the same stretch of road, one deviant can wreck *everyone's* day.

Expect people in the suburbs to be bored with driving and merely going through the motions of operating a two- or three-ton vehicle amidst the rest of the world.

A mistake (like dropping an ice cream cone in your lap and taking your eyes off the road for three seconds) that may cause no problems on a city street at 30 miles per hour can cause multiple fatalities on a busy freeway. Your goal when dealing with other drivers on the freeway is to find those who are doing something different than everyone else, and avoiding them like Superman avoids kryptonite.

Half of all motorcycle fatalities happen on roads just like this one. Don't get too overconfident when your only distractions are the blue sky and fresh air. Roads like this still have intersections, blind spots, and "pedestrians," though those are typically of the four-legged and easily startled variety.

The boondocks are beautiful, but they're no place to let your guard down on your motorcycle.

Country Roads and Two-Lane Highways

Arguably the most enticing of all roads for a motorcyclist, back roads (two-laners) also pose, statistically, the most risk to a motorcyclist. Here you have the speeds of a freeway with the rural predictability of a city street. Sure, you can see for a long way, but that only makes you lazier and less alert to hazards like tractors popping out of the farm field or dogs that cannot resist but try to get a taste of those fancy new motorcycle boots of yours. Like going for a ride and enjoying the scenery? So do half of the recreational riders who are killed on Saturdays and Sundays every year.

The boondocks are beautiful, but they're no place to let your guard down on your motorcycle. Don't get distracted by the beautiful scenery, picturesque farms, and humble villages while you're out there exploring on your motorcycle. Just like in the city, big lumbering vehicles will pull out in front of you at a moment's notice; large, unintelligent mammals will leap out onto the road; humongous, immovable objects will block your view and any hope of an emergency exit. The best roads of all—these country roads—are the most dangerous for motorcycle riders. Ride them like you'd ride city streets: hyper-aware and slow enough to react to *anything*. The more you want to sightsee, the slower you have to go. Just be careful not to hold up any tractors or horse-and-buggy combos while you're out there.

These are all general guidelines for the various roadway types you'll encounter. Every geographical area boasts different sorts of hazards and speed/predictability relationships. As a rider, you'll get good at finding your way safely through your "home turf" and you'll have your own set of guidelines for what to expect. However, when you start to explore new areas, these birds-eye views of generic traffic and roadway types will give you a good mental base from which to start.

Recommended Reading:

Proficient Motorcycling by David Hough—Probably the best, most comprehensive motorcycle safety and technique book written. It's time for you to gain some serious technical knowledge and learn how to handle the curve balls that will come your way.

www.msgroup.org—A hobbyist posted 100+ essays on various aspects of motorcycle riding: theoretical, technical, social, practical, mechanical, and historical. While much of it is researched opinion and not inarguable fact, exposure to these viewpoints will make you a more knowledgeable, well-rounded motorcyclist.

The boondocks are the greatest places to ride, but beware: The family that lives there owns at least one dog, skips off to church at a moment's notice, has to walk across the road to check the mail, and uses that beautiful strip of asphalt to take the muddy combine from field A to field B.

Every geographical area boasts different sorts of hazards and speed/predictability relationships.

GETTING BETTER

BY THIS TIME YOU WILL HAVE GOTTEN GOOD AT MAINTAINING YOUR COMPOSURE IN TRAFFIC. YOU CAN MAKE THE BIKE GO WHERE YOU WANT IT, KEEP YOURSELF FROM GETTING CAUGHT IN HIGH-DENSITY, SHARE-THE-ROAD SNARES AND "PUCKER" MOMENTS, AND YOU'RE STARTING TO GET A LITTLE BORED. BORED CAN BE GOOD.

By this I mean that you're no longer using 100 percent of your brain to ride the bike. You've got some breathing room. Your hands and feet know what to do, your instincts and training help you react to different riding situations, and you're fairly comfortable with what the road normally throws at you on any given day. What you've done is cleared space in your brain to pack more in, to learn more about riding, to grow, and to get even better at blending smoothly with the world around you.

Up until now you've intelligently avoided situations that put you at undue risk such as riding on freeways, in heavy traffic, at night, or in the rain. However, you can't and shouldn't avoid them forever. You need to learn to deal with every possible scenario you'll encounter on a motorcycle. Now you're ready to really start making some leaps in your riding ability. The way to get the most bang for your motorcycling buck is to build your mental skills. Your biggest risks at this point in your career are not the ones you create, but the ones that are created around you, so it's critical that you visualize them in advance, be ready for them, and have a plan of attack (or escape).

When you've finally got your skills to the point that operating the bike becomes almost automatic, it's time to take the next jump. To survive on a motorcycle, you need to be able to read the traffic environment, predict what will happen, and take steps to keep yourself out of harm's way. This is where you'll make the biggest advances in your ability to live a long and prosperous life as a motorcyclist.

Don't Be There

There's a great story about a karate student who was perfecting his defensive moves when he asked his teacher, "What's the best way to avoid a punch?" The teacher, a very wise and infuriatingly vague mentor, said, "The best way to avoid a punch is to *not be there*." That's about as good a piece of motorcycle advice as I've ever heard. Your goal when it comes to trouble areas is to avoid putting yourself into a bad situation in the first place.

Big Secret Number 6: "Why Crashes Happen"

I've mentioned already the concept of Motorcyclist Information Overload. Notwithstanding the very few exceptions that are best labeled acts of God, almost every motorcycle crash is a direct result of what happens when too many risk factors converge on the rider at one time. Motorcyclist Information Overload (MIO) simply means the rider's mind is not able to process all the information quickly enough to avoid a disaster.

Think of motorcycle riding as a video game like Pac-Man or Tetris. At the beginning of the game, everything moves slowly and even a fumble-fisted beginner with no depth perception *or* hand-eye coordination can hold his own. But as the game progresses and gets more advanced, everything speeds up and you need to see a broader picture, make quicker decisions, and react instantly with your hands to stay out of trouble. Riding is the same way. (Tetris, the kooky building-block puzzle game, is actually a great form of mental exercise for dealing with traffic. As you get better at it, you learn to use your peripheral vision, plan ahead, and improve your reaction times. The obstacles in the video game come at you very much like vehicles on the roadway. It's up to you to sort them out and make them fit into the overall picture. Find a $10 version of Tetris in the store or a free version on the Internet and get to practicing. Justify it as mental calisthenics.)

The best way to limit or eliminate MIO is to slow down the rate at which hazards approach. One way to do this is to slow down and ride at a speed that allows your brain to resume normal, effective information processing. While it may not always be possible or advisable to ride slower than the rest of the traffic, it's a sure-fire way to slow the world down. The additional risks you face from behind are offset by the fewer risks you face from the roadway ahead of you. When you feel your brain becoming overloaded, it's time to slow it down or take a break.

Another way to combat MIO is to remove risks from the overall equation. As I've mentioned in previous chapters, the biggest challenges a rider faces are usually the ones the rider creates for himself or herself—especially impairments like distraction, emotion, anxiety, fatigue, and alcohol. Removing these barriers to clear motorcycle thinking frees up your brain to deal with the hazards you can't remove.

Games that challenge your ability to make quick decisions and react instantly are good for your motorcycle brain, which has to absorb information constantly, sort it, and respond with intelligence and good timing.

"The best way to avoid a punch is to not be there."

One of the trickiest and most dangerous places to take a motorcycle is an intersection.

Where Roads Collide

Remember when I told you way back in Chapter 1 that the road was *designed* to make you crash? Well, here we are, we have an official case in point. But instead of lending too much personality and a nasty attitude to an inanimate asphalt slab, let's analyze and outsmart the road instead.

One of the trickiest and most dangerous places to take a motorcycle is an intersection. What makes these little roadway delights such trouble is the fact that you're using a smaller vehicle that other drivers can't see easily, in addition to being less intimidating than, say, a Mack truck with a big scary clown face on the grille. You're also more vulnerable, physically. The consequences of someone violating your right of way or ramming you from behind will be quite a bit more memorable than if you are buckled up in an SUV. To make things worse, stoplights force people to make snap-speed and timing decisions for themselves, rarely giving thought to the problems they could create if they misjudge the traffic and screw up. Think of an intersection not just as a place where two roads collide; think of it as a razor-sharp knife thrust sideways into the ribs of smoothly flowing traffic.

The wee little motorcycle doesn't impose a scary presence like the bigger vehicle does. Other drivers, less worried about motorcycles, will be more apt to pull out in front of you. You're also harder to see, which makes for double trouble. Assume you're invisible.

To a non-rider, you stand out when you're wearing motorcycle gear. Fill those lungs up, spread your arms out, and draw attention to yourself just being who you are. Making the other guy just a little bit uncomfortable to be around you might help you stand out enough to avoid a bear trap.

Not every intersection will present a hazardous situation. In fact, probably less than 1 in 10 of them will. You can usually just cruise right through when you have the green light. However, when something goes wrong in an intersection, it usually involves a moving vehicle skidding and smashing violently into a nonmoving vehicle, or one moving so slowly it's the equivalent of a brick wall. It makes good sense to prepare for the worst whenever you have roads come together. Remember, your attitude is that everyone is trying to kill you. Think of an intersection as jaws of a steel trap waiting to snap shut as you pass through.

The best place to be is in plain sight. Ride in a portion of your lane that makes you obvious to oncoming traffic and those waiting to turn. If you can't place yourself where everyone can see you, you have to continually shift positions in your lane and use movement to try to draw attention to yourself. Consider wearing a bright orange safety vest over your gear. In fact, you can even use these opportunities to work on your "aggressive animal" posture: sit up as high as you can in the seat, stick your elbows and knees out farther, take a big, deep breath and puff yourself up like a big, colorful peacock or pissed-off pussycat. (Ever seen a puffer fish?) Do whatever you can to draw extra attention to yourself, even if it may seem silly.

The best place to be is in plain sight.

Use every part of your lane to make yourself conspicuous and to give yourself lots of room side-to-side. Shift position often to draw attention to yourself.

Don't stare at any one vehicle or driver too long. Keep your eyes moving.

Reduce your speed and cover your brakes, anticipating an emergency stop. It's when you least expect it that some happy leadfoot will decide he doesn't want to wait any more and there's a big enough gap to pull out. These people usually wait until there is absolutely no way you can avoid them, then lurch into your path—and stop. Your best bet in a situation like that is to scrub off as much speed as possible, giving yourself additional time and space to react. Stop if you have to, but remember that the person behind you is probably more surprised than you are and now you have *two* problems. Slow down enough to let the moving

obstacle clear out, or if it doesn't, you can get around it with a quick swerve.

Don't stare at any one vehicle or driver too long. Keep your eyes moving. As you gain more experience riding in hazardous situations, you'll get better at reading the environment and knowing when someone is about to do something stupid. You'll

Yellow lights force people to make quick decisions. Don't get anywhere near one if you can help it.

start to pick up valuable information from your peripheral vision, which is better at detecting movement. Devise a backup plan for every situation, imagine your escape route(s), and be ready for the worst. Be prepared to aim your bike into oncoming traffic, the shoulder, the ditch, or the sidewalk if you have to. I'm serious. If you're mentally ready for it, it'll be an easier pill to swallow for that one-in-ten-thousand time when you *have* to.

Give yourself space to maneuver. Ride as close as you can to the center of your side of the road. If there's only one lane on your side, stay toward the middle of it. If there are two lanes, stick close to the white dashed line to equalize the distance between potential hazards left and right. This maximizes your options (swerve left, swerve right) should something go awry.

Yellow lights at intersections are a real problem. They cause everybody to lose their mind and make either aggressive charges or panic maneuvers. Everybody tries to do everything at once. People gun the engine and turn to clear the intersection, slam on their brakes to avoid running a red light, and stomp their gas pedal to make it through before the light changes. Pay attention to what the light's doing before you reach the intersection, an eighth- or even a quarter-mile before you get there. If it has only recently turned green, you probably have a little time before it switches to yellow. If it's been green a long time, it may be ready to change, or people waiting to pull out or turn may be getting impatient. If you're sure the light's going to change before you get there, either start slowing down or speeding up to time your arrival for a smoother crossing.

Devise a backup plan for every situation, imagine your escape route(s), and be ready for the worst.

Watch the hands on the steering wheel or the movement of the front wheel for indicators that the car is going to move.

Use it if you must, avoid it if you can. The high speeds of the freeway combined with the poor perception and skills of typical drivers can create a motorcycle-eating machine. The side roads are much more fun anyway—stick to those.

Enthusiast riders generally avoid the freeway when they can. It's a lot more fun to stick to the curvy side roads and little mom-and-pop gas stations.

The Superslab

So-named for the enormous hulk of concrete pad it brings to mind, the super-slab is what motorcyclists refer to as the freeway. Designed to move lots of traffic in a hurry, it holds many problems—and few solutions—for the unwary motorcycle rider. Freeways combine high speed and heavy traffic that wants to keep flowing no matter what happens. When things go wrong, the conflict can set off a chain reaction that causes problems way down the road.

Enthusiast riders generally avoid the freeway when they can. It's a lot more fun to stick to the curvy side roads, and little mom-and-pop gas stations and restaurants are a lot more interesting than roadside fast-food and gas superstations. Freeways seldom offer much in the way of scenery, while forgotten county roads (sometimes shadowing the freeway) are a lot more fun, even though they move slower and take longer to get from point A to B.

Instead of intersections, on freeways you're forced to deal with merging areas like on-ramps and off-ramps. These are a

little more predictable than most intersections, but a lot faster. Most earth-lings, as a rule, simply do not "get it" that the purpose of these ramps is acceleration and deceleration so incoming and outgoing traffic can make smooth transitions on and off the freeway. Instead, problem drivers try to wedge themselves into the flow at the speed *they* feel like traveling. They attempt to blend with 65-mile-per-hour traffic at 50 miles per hour, plus speed demons are behind them, right on their tail, which forces everyone to accommodate two (or more) vehicles merging instead of just one. This causes everyone in the right lane to slam on their brakes to make room, everyone on the ramp to slam on their brakes, and everybody has to bunch up. This ugly mess of a result can hold up traffic for miles. To make matters worse, while all this is going on, everyone in the right-hand lane was already following too closely anyway, not leaving enough space for even one car to join the conga line. It's like some sort of weird metal rodeo.

When dealing with merge areas, allow plenty of space between you and the vehicle in front of you so traffic can come together smoothly. It's a simple matter of cooperation: if everyone left enough room for one vehicle, human turn-taking behavior would rule and merging would be graceful and efficient. When you're on an entrance ramp, try to match the speed of the prevailing traffic before moving into it. If you're exiting, wait until you're out of the flow to do your heavy braking. Signal your intentions well in advance, and give everyone a little extra time and patience to adapt to your presence. When you're on the freeway and approaching merge areas, use extra caution, anticipate that there will be problems, and try to avoid the problem area by using the center or left lane.

Because of the higher speeds associated with freeways, it takes more time and space for drivers to react. If something goes wrong up ahead of you, you're hurtling toward it at 55 miles per hour or more instead of 30 miles per hour. Making matters worse, because the controlled access makes the superslabs so much more "predictable" than other roads, drivers get lazy and complacent—especially on rural interstates. When something like a stray deer, a blown tractor-trailer tire, or a forgotten couch makes its appearance on the concrete stage, all hell breaks loose.

Instead of watching 4–8 seconds ahead of you like on the smaller, slower roads, scan 15–30 seconds ahead. That's a quarter to a half a mile at freeway speeds. Use your peripheral vision to keep track of what's going on close to you. This allows you to get a big-picture view of what's happening out there and provides you a great deal of time to recognize a bad situation before it becomes *your* bad situation. Expect problems to come from merge areas and abnormally slow or fast drivers. You should take special care to make mirror checks and over-the-shoulder head checks frequently (every 7-15 seconds or so). They won't be necessary 99 times out of 100, but the one time it is necessary, the butt you save will be your own.

Because the superslab is a little bit more predictable, pay very close attention to anything out of the ordinary—any deviation from the norm, no matter how small. If you see brake lights flash a tenth of a mile ahead of you, there's probably a reason. Move away from that area of the road. If you notice someone is drifting around in their lane or speeding up and slowing down, expect that that driver is going to cause a problem. Put some distance between them and you. When you see a vehicle broken down on the shoulder, expect it to jump back out into traffic from a standing start or attempt some disastrous U-turn. At freeway speeds, you can't afford any mistakes.

Instead of watching 4–8 seconds ahead of you like on the smaller, slower roads, scan 7-15 seconds ahead. That's a quarter- to a half-mile at freeway speeds.

On the superslab, you can increase your line of sight to spot problems up to a half-mile away. Don't get lazy and trap yourself by watching only three or four seconds ahead.

When the Road Gets Crowded

As a dedicated motorcyclist, you'll eventually find yourself in heavy traffic. Roads are designed to flow a certain number of cars at a certain rate. During rush hours or other times of dense traffic, more vehicles are crammed onto the roadway than it can safely handle. Everyone still wants to go as fast as they would on an empty road, so the road will suddenly accommodate fewer mistakes. Escape routes become smaller. Following distances tighten up. Space cushions disappear. And no matter how futile it is, there's always at least one bonehead aggressive driver who'll put everyone else's lives on the line to get to their somewhere a little sooner.

What makes this type of traffic even worse is that it usually occurs during rush hour, meaning most other drivers are preoccupied with either getting to work or getting home—not with driving the car. A rider needs to stay absolutely focused on the task at hand while simultaneously realizing that no one else is paying much attention.

Even on a bike, heavy traffic is no fun. Avoid it. If you're not comfortable in close quarters, pick some other time to ride. If you have no choice, at least find a route that offers you a little more room to work. Consider wearing an obnoxious orange or yellow reflective safety vest over your riding gear. Do whatever else you can to be conspicuous, keep careful track of every vehicle within two seconds of you, and do not let yourself get distracted. Keep your eyes and your brain moving. And remember, while lane splitting is illegal in most states, in an emergency it may be the only way to save your banana; a bike is smaller and can squirt into or through gaps that larger vehicles can't. Remember what I told you in Chapter 1, that a motorcycle can have a *huge* edge in traffic, if only the rider knows how to wield that advantage.

Consider wearing an obnoxious orange or yellow reflective safety vest over your riding gear. Do whatever else you can to be conspicuous, keep careful track of every vehicle within two seconds of you, and do not let yourself get distracted.

How many times have you been halfway home from work without even realizing how you got there? During rush hours, most people are thinking about where they just were or where they're going, but rarely thinking hard about where they are. Do you even see *the motorcyclists in this picture? Hint: Neither do they.*

Good gear often comes with bright strips of reflective material, but visually, a motorcyclist at night doesn't offer much to catch the inattentive driver's attention.

There's little you can do about animals and drunk drivers other than to assume there's one around every corner.

After Hours, After Dark

If you have the choice, avoid riding at night altogether. We've already established that riding is 90 percent mental, and the information you need to stay safe is 90 percent visual. Riding after dark places you at a distinct disadvantage. If you want to explore the world on your motorcycle during night-time hours (and lots of talented riders do), you have to be willing to take on additional risks: poor visibility, large jumpy animals, and drunk drivers. As scary as all this might seem, there are still ways to do it in relative safety.

Most important is to have a spotless eye protection free of scratches, bugs, and dirt. You need every ounce of vision you can get your hands on. On a motorcycle, your eyes are more important than everyone else's. Think about it this way: who'd live longer, a blindfolded

motorcyclist riding around in traffic, or a motorcyclist with perfect vision riding around in blindfolded traffic? Alcohol and fatigue can affect your vision dramatically, so make sure you're physically up to the task. Brightly colored protective gear with plenty of retroreflective materials can go a long way to getting you noticed.

There's little you can do about animals and drunk drivers other than to assume there's one around every corner. Remember that deer like to move at dawn and dusk during spring green-up and fall mating season. When riding at night, keep other, larger vehicles in front of you to act as blockers and also so you can scan ahead to see what they see in their headlights. Think hard about what attracts drunk drivers (bars, sporting events, holidays) and pay close attention when conditions are ripe.

To be prepared for the worst, you'll need some storage on your bike for things like clothing, water, and rain gear. Saddlebags mean that stuff's always with you if you want it. Portable tank bags mean you don't have to leave it on the bike.

Experienced, thoughtful riders have a saying about this: "If it's too hot to wear the gear, it's too hot to ride."

Weather You Like It or Not

Some riders claim they don't need bad-weather gear because they don't ride in bad weather. That's all well and good until they get caught in a surprise downpour on their way home from work! The first time is a real eye-opener. Exposed to the environment as motorcyclists are, weather can cause serious problems for the unprepared. Extremes of heat and cold can catch a rider off guard and send him or her tumbling into the realms of dehydration or hypothermia without the rider even realizing it. Temperature also affects the motorcycle's traction, sometimes for better, sometimes for worse. Rain and other types of condensation can be very distracting and reduce visibility as well as traction. A rider's best solution for these problems is preparation and awareness.

Wind drains your body's moisture and temperature by evaporating sweat and cooling the skin while you ride. On hot days you may not even notice that you're sweating, because the wind evaporates your sweat instantly, keeping you dry and cool . . . for a while. Riders need to keep replenishing their water whether they feel they need to or not. On the other side of the coin, cool air can reduce your body temperature dramatically—but you don't realize that you're thinking in slow motion until it's too late. Traffic starts to happen around you and your synapses can't fire quick enough to keep up. Eventually, a hazard will bear down on you before you are able to perceive it and your ride is *over*. Even on a dry day that seems warm enough, at 65 degrees, the effect of the wind chill takes it down to about 40 degrees. A couple of hours riding around in that and you're a Popsicle at the controls—probably dehydrated, too. Yikes.

Without riding gear, you're at the mercy of the environment. Exposed skin on a hot, sunny day can also net you a terrific sunburn that you won't feel until you've stopped riding. Good gear minimizes the effects of hot, cold, and dry air by insulating you to some degree and regulating the rate at which your body loses water and heat. Even on the hottest days, don't leave home without it. Experienced, thoughtful riders have a saying about this: "If it's too hot to wear

the gear, it's too hot to ride." Truer words are seldom spoken. If it's too hot, that's what cars and air conditioning are for.

The best way to deal with poor weather is to be prepared, mentally and physically, to deal with it on your own terms. Heat and cold are easy enough to handle. Dress in layers when it's cold, carry spare clothing when it's hot, and always have water or sports drinks at hand when you're out on your bike. A rain suit can keep you dry in a downpour, and it makes an excellent wind barrier in the cold. Hardcore riders use heated clothing that plugs right into the bike's battery to keep extra warm when the temps drop below about 45 degrees. A well-prepared rider with gear for every one of Mother Nature's moods can extend his or her riding season by two months or more! Want more time to ride? Buy better gear.

When it rains, everything changes on a motorcycle. Rain is distracting both to the rider and everyone else on the road. On a motorcycle, you'll feel as if everything's closing in on you, and if you're not used to wearing gear, your rain suit will probably make you feel claustrophobic. Wet fingers and face can make it difficult to pay close attention to the world around you and to operate the bike with any precision. Other drivers become sealed up in their bubbles, isolated from the elements and the sounds of the road, and hypnotized by the back-and-forth of the wipers. Motorcyclists are hard enough to see in the best of conditions; they're nearly invisible on gray, rainy days. This is when a superbright safety vest or bright yellow riding gear comes in very handy. Traction deteriorates, too: Wet pavement is only good for about half the traction of dry pavement, and in the first 20 minutes or so of a rainstorm, the road is as slippery as ice while the accumulated dirt and oil is washed from the surface.

Motorcyclists are hard enough to see in the best of conditions; they're nearly invisible on gray, rainy days. This is when a superbright safety vest or bright yellow riding gear comes in very handy.

Serious riders all have some kind of rain gear that they carry with them wherever they go. Get some. And instead of waiting for it to rain on your parade, get out there and try it out right away, in a "safe" place, to start building your wet-weather motorcycle skills and comfort level.

You'll be happier and more energized, and your coworkers will look at you in a whole new light, when you show up on a motorcycle every day. Enjoy it. Be patient with their weird looks and questions. Make it a point to seem extra friendly and extra happy.

Most carpool or high-occupancy vehicle (HOV) lanes allow motorcycles. And the social good you do by taking up less space in traffic, guzzling fewer gallons of gas, and showing the world that you're a serious, dedicated motorcyclist far outweighs the extra effort it takes to get ready in the morning.

Commuting

What separates recreational motorcyclists from diehards is the giving up of comfort and the bucking of the convention of a car and commuting on two wheels. This is a great way to bump your skills up a notch and find some extra time during the day to spend riding. What's more, you arrive at work with a smile on your face and have a great way to unwind after a hard day at the salt mines. But beware—unless you're very comfortable on your bike in rush-hour traffic, commuting may be too much on your new rider's brain. Start with one day a week, then ride more often as you get used to it.

Motorcycle commuters are a different breed. They don't mind arriving at work with their hair a little rumpled and wearing clothes that don't quite fit in with "business casual." They often park their helmets where important memos should go, change clothes in their cube, and walk around the office all day in motorcycle boots. If this sounds appealing to you, welcome to the world of the workaday motorcyclist.

Riding to work not only starts your day off right, it has other benefits, too. Gas is cheaper because a motorcycle uses less. Parking is easier because bikes use less space—indeed, many companies try to encourage employees to ride to work by providing secure parking close to the doors. Most carpool or high-occupancy vehicle (HOV) lanes allow motorcycles. And the social good you do by taking up less space in traffic, guzzling fewer gallons of gas, and showing the world that you're a serious, dedicated motorcyclist far outweighs the extra effort it takes to get ready in the morning. People may look at you funny in the elevator in your leathers, but eventually they'll come to realize someone they know and respect rides a motorcycle, and that maybe they should pay a little more attention on the road.

Commuting places a few hurdles in your path. The biggest one is switching daily from sleepy breakfast mind to riding mind, then from riding mind to working mind, then from working mind back to riding mind for the trip home, without letting the details of work creep into your consciousness while you're on your bike. That's a lot of transitions to make. Smart commuters take a little extra time in the morning to mentally prepare themselves for the ride in to work and visualize their route, keeping in mind that everyone else will be half asleep or munching donuts in traffic. Before hopping on the bike and heading home, savvy riders take a few extra minutes to relax, forget about the workday, mentally plan out their route home, and then work hard to concentrate on riding the bike when what their brain really wants to think about is that cold beer waiting in the fridge. Beware of riding on stressful days. I spend some days thinking my brain off,

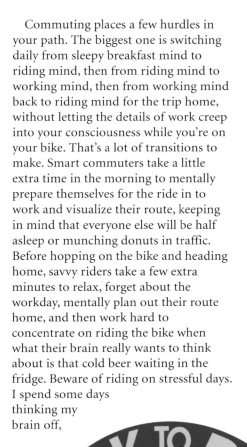

and I'm exhausted at quitting time, as well as still tangled up in the problems I was trying to solve all day. I ride home slowly when I feel like that, many times taking a different (longer!) route home to avoid the rut and just unwind.

Overall, you don't save a ton of time riding to work. You may get the benefit of using the carpool lane or finding a better, closer parking place, which will help offset the extra work. But it does takes a little longer to get all geared up than it does to just jump in the car. You have to pack everything you may need along with you. And you have to be prepared for any kind of weather, which means you have to pack even more stuff along with you. Riding every day means you get every different kind of weather, sometimes all in the same day. Cold in spring and fall, morning and evening, hot in summer, rainy a day or two a week, windy a day or two a week, and for at least a couple of weeks a year, you get to ride right into the rising or setting sun. (If you're salivating while you're reading this, you're already a commuter and you don't even know it.) While average recreational riders try to be prepared for anything in general, commuters try to be prepared for anything every day. It's a lot of work, but it's worth it.

If you ride a motorcycle, you should commute: At least according to the nonprofit organization Ride to Work (www.ridetowork.org). Lauding the social benefits of motorcycles for transportation, the Web site alone is good for hours of motorcycle-related reading. Plus, they're good people. Enjoy.

If you're salivating while you're reading this, you're already a commuter and you don't even know it.

A Couple of New Tricks

Running Errands

Face it, it's cool to drop in to your local hardware store on your motorcycle and wander the aisles decked out in your motorcycle gear. When you're able to commute to work and stay focused even after the worst of days, you're ready to start making milk runs on your bike. By now your car is probably sitting on four flat tires and gathering dust because you take your bike everywhere you go.

One of the most telling findings in the 1981 Hurt Study was that 90 percent of all crashes happen within the first hour of riding and 50 percent happen within the first six *minutes*. Just like hopping on the bike after a hard day of work, before you hop on the bike for a quick jaunt up to the library or beer store, you need to take a few moments to focus on your route and your plan. Mentally, you need to separate the errand from the ride. Worry about what you need to pick up at the store before you leave, or after you get there. But while you're riding, you're riding and focusing on the ride only, just like you did when you were first learning. You have to be totally on the ball to get away with making short trips on your motorcycle without tripping up and landing on your face.

You have to be totally on the ball to get away with making short trips on your motorcycle without tripping up and landing on your face.

Whenever you're in the neighborhood, make it a point to drop in on your grandma with your bike and all your gear. Grandmas usually love visitors, their opinions of motorcyclists will get better as they learn more about your new passion, and they'll probably tell their grandma friends, too. More points for the good guys.

When you're recognizable as a motorcyclist and doing the stuff normal people do, people begin to recognize motorcyclists as . . . normal people. Shake things up a little bit, relish the funny looks people give you, and show those earthlings how much more fun you're having than they are.

Nights Out

Like commuting and running errands, another way to use your bike for reasons other than riding is to take it with you when you make social calls. Nonmotorcyclists are almost always surprised and curious when someone shows up for a party or at a bar on a bike. They stand out in a crowd in their gear. They buck convention by pulling right up to the homeowner's garage or parking on the sidewalk. And they conspicuously turn down refreshments like beer, wine, or mixed drinks and instead wet their whistles with soda, lemonade, or iced tea. (People are then probably asking themselves, "What's so great about motorcycling that they'd skip happy hour drinks?")

Again, the trick is to separate the riding from the social event. You're heading out to have fun, but to get there, you still have to handle the road and all the usual riding problems. Think it through. Think about where you'll park when you get there. Plan on having your fun without alcohol. Also, plan your departure time, imagining the route home in the dark, so you're prepared for that, too. You don't want to be riding home when you're really tired and the sharpness of your eyes and brain are done for the day. Remember that there will be lots of other drivers out there

heading home, too—and not all of them have been enjoying their "sophisticated adult refreshments" in moderation.

A Word about Alcohol

Most people are smart enough to know when to say "when," but many new or returning riders have been driving a car for a long time. They're comfortable in the knowledge that they can have a drink or two and still be legal to drive. Many riders, especially those born before 1970, grew up in a time when drinking and driving a car was relatively acceptable. Because they don't feel dramatically different after a couple of loudmouth cocktails than they do normally, they think they're okay to drive. Maybe so.

But on a bike it's very, very different. The skills required to ride are quite a bit more advanced, and the subtle effects of alcohol—even the effects of one drink—start chipping away at your judgment, vision, and inhibitions all while sneakily building up your confidence. This is a Bad Combination. After only a few drinks your physical abilities, like hand-eye coordination and small muscle control, get sloppy and because your judgment is already impaired, you don't realize it at all—another Bad Combination. Riding is fun enough without drinking. Drinking is fun enough without riding. If you're in the mood to be a motorcycle enthusiast, avoid alcohol at all costs. Even one drink an hour

(an ordinarily good rule of thumb) can be too much. It's not worth the risk. If you're in the mood to be a drinking enthusiast, just stay off the bike. Leave it at home and hitch a ride with somebody else.

Errands and nights out on a motorcycle are important in the same way that riding to work is important: It exposes nonriders to the fact that motorcycle riders are human beings that they know and like. Standing in line at the grocery store in your leathers with your helmet in hand, or standing at a bar drinking iced tea while your friends drink beer allows ordinary people to get a glimpse of what motorcyclists really are: people, just like them, yet somehow more . . . mysterious. When they see you often enough, acting normal and looking friendly, they may just start treating all motorcyclists differently. They might even start becoming curious about trying riding for themselves. Score another couple of points for the good guys.

Recommended Reading:

A Twist of the Wrist by Keith Code— A legendary book focused on motorcycle racing techniques. Imaginative riders and readers can use the information to great advantage on the street.

Total Control by Lee Parks—A book showcasing advanced street-riding techniques that focus on control and skill development, with drills to help you improve.

Plan on having your fun without alcohol.

Many people consider motorcycling recreational. Many people consider drinking recreational. Some people like to combine their two favorite activities so they can have twice as much fun. People, the ride is intoxicating enough. If you ride, don't drink. If you drink, don't ride. It's that simple.

What People Say and What People Mean Number 6: "There're Two Kinds of Riders..."

" . . . Those who have gone down, and those who will."

This is an enormous pile of flapdoodle, another example of someone trying to prove how wise they are and how much they know about motorcycling. They're *conning* you. Lots of riders out there have never crashed and never will. There are no absolutes when it comes to motorcycling.

You can be a completely idiotic, drunken, speeding maniac and never even come close to crashing your bike. On the other hand, no matter how smart you are, how skilled you are, and how great your attitude, you can still get tangled up in traffic—or in the middle of nowhere, on your own—and put that motorcycle in a very upside-down and bashed-up sort of way. But saying you've either crashed or you will crash is a load of hooey.

Or is it?

Look at it from the perspective of attitude, and it takes on a whole new life. Thinking back to Chapter one, the three attitudes riders need to survive are:

• You are responsible for everything that happens on the road.

• All other drivers are trying to kill you.

• The road is designed to make you crash.

Now, we know that none of these things can possibly be true, but we agree that it's in a rider's best interest to pretend that they are true. This new one is no different. If you assume that you will eventually crash someday, you'll always take measures to try to keep that from happening. This keeps you fresh, keeps you learning, and keeps you honest about yourself and your abilities. To keep beating this dead, belabored horse, it is the rider's *attitude* that makes the biggest difference in his or her survival, and this "Those who have and those who will" saying is another great example of good rider attitude, whether the know-it-all utterer realizes it or not.

So add a fourth attitude to your general approach to riding:

• There are two kinds of riders: Those who have crashed, and those who will.

Tattoo it on you arm if you have to. Motorcyclists have to think—and live—differently than everybody else. Photo by Dean Groover.

If you assume that you will eventually crash someday, you'll always take measures to try to keep that from happening.

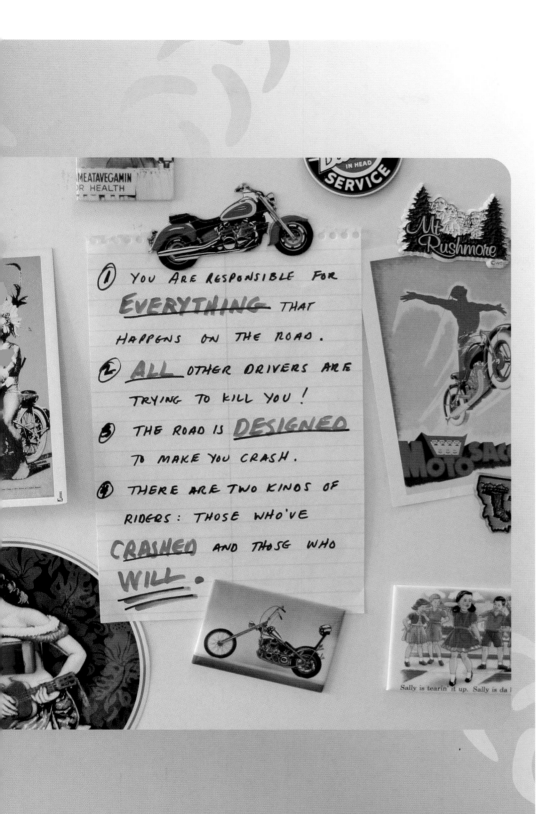

To keep beating this dead, belabored horse, it is the *rider's* attitude *that makes the biggest difference in his or her survival…*

GETTING INVOLVED

BY THE TIME YOU REACH THIS STAGE IN YOUR DEVELOPMENT AS A MOTORCYCLIST, YOU'VE SURPASSED MOST OF THE RIDERS OUT THERE IN SKILL AND KNOWLEDGE. IT'S NO SMALL FEAT THAT GOT YOU HERE; IT WAS A LOT OF EFFORT, A LOT OF SACRIFICE AND SELF-CONTROL, A LOT OF PRACTICE, AND A FAIR AMOUNT OF LUCK.

You have reached the most elusive part of motorcycling, the deepest, coolest, and most difficult-to-see bottom of the proverbial iceberg. Now it's time to reap the rewards of a smart, solid riding foundation. You're not only going to get more out of motorcycling, you're also going to start giving *back*.

There are as many ways to enjoy motorcycling as there are motorcycles. You'll find that once you achieve a certain level of proficiency, you'll be looking for ways to expand your motorcycling interests. When it comes to riding enthusiasm, you could have "the world" and sometimes still want more. There's probably a dream bike you've been thinking about for a while. It may no longer be enough to just ride by yourself. You may decide you want to ride with a passenger or in a group. You may want to get some advanced training, or join a club. If you're really ambitious, you may even decide to try your hand at teaching others to ride. And you'll be able to do all these things, because at this point in your riding evolution, you'll have the basic tools you need to take that next step.

If you're not careful, motorcycling can consume you. When you buy a new house, the garage may be your biggest selling point. When you have somewhere to be, it's not whether or not you should ride there, but which bike you should take. When people ask you if you have any hobbies, you're hard-pressed to think of any—riding has gone beyond a pastime and become a lifestyle.

Trading Up

Oh, this is the best part. You've probably spent a year or two mastering the controls, getting your feet wet in traffic, learning the ropes of maintenance, and riding the wheels off your first bike. Now you're feeling pretty adept at making the motorcycle do what you want . . . but your first bike doesn't do certain things as well as you'd like. Maybe you'd like to ride longer and need a little more comfort and storage capacity, or a larger tank and longer legs. Maybe you've discovered that your heart longs to slowly cruise every inch of your stomping grounds, turning heads and taking in the sights and listening to the rumble of those cubic centimeters. You may have had a taste of some twisting country roads and are thinking about getting a bike that can ride those corners the way a dolphin rides waves. You're ready to take everything you've learned about riding and use it to pick out your dream bike.

To make your best purchase, you have to first decide what you liked, and what you didn't like, about your first bike. Was it too tall or too short? Was it too heavy or too light? How was the riding position? Did you like the reach to the handlebars, the bent riding position of your legs, and the weight distribution? What about the fuel range? Do you want something geared toward long distances? Did your motorcycle have enough power, or do you want to dig into something bigger, stronger, or faster? Did it stop the way you thought it should? Did it corner too easily, or did it take too much work to get it leaned over? How did you feel on longer trips? Did your butt or your wrists get sore, or did the vibration make your hands and feet numb? What about wind? Did you feel protected or were you constantly fighting to hold yourself upright, wearing out your back and your arms?

To make your best purchase, you have to first decide what you liked, and what you didn't like, about your first bike.

Each of these bikes represents a specialized class of motorcycle, and none are suitable for newbies. After a year or two, when you've learned everything you can on your first motorcycle, it's okay to step up to a more focused bike and start expanding your horizons, both literally and figuratively. Courtesy Yamaha Motor Corp., BMW, and Kawasaki.

You've wisely avoided adding any unnecessary distractions to your ride, but now you're ready to take on a passenger. While carrying passengers isn't much riskier than riding alone, pillions do affect the way your bike handles, so you'll need to relearn some of your skills to accommodate the extra weight—and accommodate your passenger's safety. Courtesy Kawasaki.

A passenger is just as vulnerable in traffic as the rider, in theory, so you incur added responsibility because now you're "riding for two."

Ask yourself all these questions and then start your research. You've probably got a pretty good idea of what style of bike you want: standard, cruiser, dual-sport, or sportbike. But as you move away from beginner-friendly bikes and into the world of too many choices, you'll also be offered machines with labels like muscle bikes, retro-cruisers, café racers, sport-standards, touring bikes, sport-touring bikes, and adventure tourers. These bikes all have specific purposes, and suit specialized tastes and expectations very well, but at the cost of sacrificing other abilities.

Another question you're going to have to ask yourself: What to do with the old bike? Some riders will tell you to keep it for old times' sake and as a backup bike. It's not unreasonable to think your spouse or kids or brother-in-law will catch motorcycle fever someday as well, and after all, it *was* a great bike to learn on. While those are good reasons to keep it, the problem is your trusty old steed will probably look kind of forlorn sitting in the garage most of the time, collecting dust and rust, and costing valuable garage real estate.

A better solution is to "recycle" your first bike. Shine it up and sell it off to another newbie motorcyclist so he or she can have the same great learning experience you did. Too many beginners get discouraged with the used bike market and resort to buying a first bike that's too big, too heavy, and too powerful for them. The consequences of their bad decisions are seen on TV, in the motorcycle junkyards, and in your insurance rates. It may hurt a little bit to part with your trusty two-wheeled friend, but you'll get a little taste of what it means to give something back to motorcycling.

Carrying Passengers

Riding two-up is the way single-track minds get to ride more, enhance personal relationships, and build new relationships and good PR among nonriders.

During your formative years, you wisely kept motorcycling to yourself. It's one thing to head out into the world as a newbie on a bike. You prepare as best you can and accept the risks for yourself. It's quite another to pile someone onto the back of your bike, and in so doing, pile additional risks on, too. A passenger is just as vulnerable in traffic as the rider, in theory, so you incur added responsibility because now you're "riding for two." A mistake with a passenger costs double. In reality, the added weight and distraction a pillion brings to the table means you'll need to hone your skills even further to deal with the new challenges. Carrying an extra 100 to 200 pounds means your bike will require more effort to steer, accelerate slower, and take more effort to stop. Passengers dramatically affect the stability of the bike, especially if they're not familiar with motorcycles. Mentally, you'll have to divide your attention to some degree to monitor your passenger's comfort, attention, and reactions. It takes a great deal more skill and attention to ride smoothly with a friend on the back.

Pillion: Passenger on a motorcycle.

But carrying a pillion means you no longer have to leave your spouse or family at home when you ride. You can share the thrills and chills of motorcycling together, which means that you may get to ride longer and more often. Even better, you'll be spending quality time with your family doing something that you love, which can bring you closer and promote a healthier, more active family life. Who knows, you may have so much fun that your Significant Other or kids decide they want a bike of their own.

Sharing a motorcycle ride with another person may even have a positive effect on the riding environment itself. While the biker stereotype of a lone rogue thumbing his or her nose at society can instill fear in the hearts of grandmothers, lawmakers, and shopkeepers, seeing a grandma and grandpa or a father and daughter riding together on a beautiful summer evening might help soften the image that motorcyclists have. It might even lead people to believe that bikers aren't all drug-snorting scofflaws intent on scattering pedestrians on the sidewalk, but human beings with friends and families and relationships that are just as important as everyone else's. Riding with a passenger is another social good, and another way to bring out the best in motorcycling. Score more points for the good guys.

Riding with a passenger is another social good, and another way to bring out the best in motorcycling.

You're going to need to lay down some more money for good motorcycle gear for your passenger. If it's going to be the same person every time, the choices are easier and you'll probably have some "help" in selecting. If you're considering multiple onboard partners, you may have to buy some more generic sizes or multiple outfits to fit multiple pillions. Every rider should have a helmet that fits as perfectly as yours—don't skimp and ask an extra small-sized head to wear an extra large-sized helmet, and don't fall into the trap of using old helmets to save money. A properly fitted helmet will make your passenger more comfortable and his or her ride more enjoyable.

Until your passenger is 100 percent comfortable—100 percent—and trusts you completely, you have to ride at their comfort level. If it's the first time they've been on a bike, think back to your comfort level the first time you were on a bike, and ride accordingly. A frightened passenger can make even a short, slow ride dangerous. And a bad experience can sour a potential riding partner on motorcycles forever.

Take it very, very easy the first few times you ride with a passenger, until you get used to the bizarre and sometimes frightening turn-in behavior.

Passenger Accommodations

Essentially, adding a passenger means you're going to make your bike less stable, more top-heavy, and give it a rear-wheel weight bias. By taking on a pillion, you're probably doubling the weight your bike has to carry and putting it way up high, and in back. Every movement that person makes, every breath he or she takes, you can feel in the motorcycle's stability and handling. Be prepared for it. Start, stop, shift, and turn more gradually.

The bike will take more effort to stop, but because most of the additional weight is on the rear wheel, the rear brake will be much more help than normal. It's a good idea to short-shift to avoid the embarrassing and amateurish helmet clunk (almost always the fault of the rider, not the passenger!) and work to be extremely smooth with your clutch and throttle transitions. Your motorcycle will require more handlebar input to get leaned over for a turn, but once it starts leaning, the added

weight and higher center of gravity will make it feel as if it wants to "flop over." At slow speeds, you may not be able to recover a bike that's gone over too far. Take it very, very easy the first few times you ride with a passenger, until you get used to the bizarre and sometimes frightening turn-in behavior. Low speed maneuvers in the driveway or parking lot require a great deal of skill to keep it smooth and balanced—and fun.

Take the time before you go ride to establish at least two nonverbal signals between you and your passenger for "slow down" and "stop." For example, your passenger should use simultaneous soft pats with both hands on the tops of your thighs for "slow down" and slightly harder alternating thigh pats (left-right-left-right) for "stop now." Or something like that, make up your own signals. However you do it, it's important that the communications, whatever they are, do not interfere with your concentration.

Short-Shifting: Intentionally shifting earlier than required for smoother shifts.

Helmet Clunk: The Three Stooges-esqe comical bonking together of helmeted heads when the operator is not smooth with the controls.

The passenger's job is to allow the rider to concentrate and not destabilize the motorcycle.

(Above) Before taking on the additional weight of a passenger, consult your owner's manual to know the maximum load the bike can carry and the recommended tire pressure. The most common reason for tire failure is underinflation; the tire pressure must increase as the weight on the bike increases. Adjust the bike's suspension and pay attention to the gross vehicle weight rating (GVWR), which is the maximum combined weight of the bike with a full tank of gas, rider and passenger, riding gear, and luggage.

(Below) The passenger and rider should lean together as one unit. The pillion keeps a firm grip (waist, hips, or grab rails) and sits far enough back to keep from crowding the operator.

Advice for the Passenger

The passenger's job is to allow the rider to concentrate and not destabilize the motorcycle. Every movement the passenger makes—every head turn, butt readjustment, or panicked "driver-grab"—will cause the bike to shift position and balance, and can cause the rider to lose concentration. The fewer there are of these types of movements, the better. Any change of position should be as smooth and unobtrusive as possible. Passengers should only communicate with the rider when absolutely necessary. It's a good idea to devise signals before the ride for such important items as "Need bathroom break," "Butt's sore," or "Do that again, wiseguy, and I'm going to wring your neck."

Experienced passengers can make the ride better and safer. Having an extra pair of eyes and ears means extra help detecting problems. A pillion can play navigator with a map in an unfamiliar area, allowing the pilot to concentrate on the road and watch for hazards. Simple signals such as the "leg-pat and thumb-point" can indicate when a turn is coming up or when an ice cream cone is no longer an option but a requirement. A passenger can pick up cold drinks and pay at the counter while the rider is pumping gas.

Like in any sport or hobby, it takes all kinds. There'll be purists and heathens, enthusiasts and hedonists, smart riders . . . and those who are not so smart. They all have at least one thing in common! Motorcycle riders are the minority out there: 1 in 10, if you believe the statistics. You've got to stick together no matter what your differences in riding style or choice of motorcycle. Be ready to learn, and to teach, when it comes to riding with others. Most of all, have fun—you have a lot more in common with these people than you do with the rest of the world.

Safety in numbers also means that you have more of a presence on the road.

Group Riding

For your first couple of years, it's in your best interest to avoid riding in a group of three or more bikes. Multiple friends on multiple bikes can be a hoot of a good time, building friendships, exploring unfamiliar roads, learning new tricks and techniques by watching and talking to other riders, and getting firsthand owner feedback on different bikes, riding gear, and restaurants. But beware the pitfalls of group riding. Added distractions, varying ability and attitude, the tendency of some riders to intrude on others' space, and the tendency of most riders to ride over their head in a group can make riding *en masse* dangerous, even to experienced motorcyclists.

But there will eventually come a time when you're invited to join a group ride. You may even organize one yourself. Why? Because it's fun, and motorcyclists from all walks of life find something in common out on the open road. It's a great way to meet people and share your experience with those above you or below you on the learning curve. Group rides also offer safety in numbers. That is, when you're out exploring the countryside and you have a mechanical problem or (gasp!) an unintentional dismount, you have friends there to get you rolling again or call for help. Safety in numbers also means that you have more of a presence on the road: You're more visible to other drivers as a group and command a little more respect than a lone rider. For both of these reasons, you could argue that riding in a group might actually be safer. Another way to look at it: Have you heard of those ridiculous animal lovers who throw buckets of red paint on 50-year-old women wearing fur? Ever heard of one of these idealists trying a stunt like this on a bunch of bikers wearing leather? Neither have I.

What to Expect

Looking through the risk-averse window of reality, we also see that the perks that make group rides great can also wreck 'em. With a "variety pack" of riders, you'll also get a variety pack of attitudes and varying levels of experience and ability. For every rider who thinks gloves and a helmet are essential for a good ride, there's a rider who thinks that "All that crap just gets in the way" and takes away from the enjoyment. For every rider who thinks that American iron is the only way to go, there's a rider out there who thinks American-made bikes are too heavy, slow, and unreliable to be worth the big price tag. For every rider dressed like a pro with the skills and experience to match, there'll be a rider with a great bike and expensive gear who's never ridden more than 50 miles at a shot and wouldn't know countersteering if it sprang up out of the bushes and chewed a hole through his or her expensive leather pants.

Instead of preparing you for every possibility (or eventuality) of group riding, let's look at it from a more positive perspective. How would *you* do it? Let's set our expectations in reverse, and evaluate group rides from our own viewpoint:

Know the rules. Every group, if they're smart, will lay down at least a few ground rules at the start of the ride regarding speed, passing, space cushioning, etc. Decide what you think is safest and remind the group that they're your guests and that bad behavior will not be tolerated. If someone wants to ride like a complete wanker, they can do it without the group.

Ride your own ride. Stay within your limits. Check your ego at the door. Regardless of what the rules are, you are still the only one responsible for your safety. Do NOT fall into the trap of trying to keep up with a fast group to impress them. Ride at the speed at which you're comfortable and in control. Groups are far more impressed by riders that know their limits than those who toss them out the window—and crash.

Stay out of your mirrors. Your goal is to have fun and ride safely. You can't do that when you're constantly staring into your rearview mirrors to see if A) a faster rider wants to pass you, or B) a slower rider has been left in the dust. Concentrate on the road ahead and check your mirrors only every seven seconds or so. And just glance—don't stare. If you need to stare, pull over and stop before you do.

Every group, if they're smart, will lay down at least a few ground rules at the start of the ride regarding speed, passing, space cushioning, etc. Decide what you think is safest and remind the group that they're your guests and that bad behavior will not be tolerated.

If a group makes a two-second-following-distance rule, remember that two seconds is a minimum following distance. There's no reason to ride in a rigid formation, no matter what the "road captain" may tell you. If the group requires a formation that you think is unsafe, find another group. Give yourself the space that you need to ride, and never follow another rider closer than he or she is following the rider in front of them.

The biggest difference between the BRC and the ERC is that you use your own bike. You're no longer learning to ride a motorcycle, you're building skills on the bike that you spend the most time riding.

The MSF Experienced Rider Course (ERC) is a great way to blow out the winter cobwebs.

Back to School

While not always easy to find, and rarely cheap, advanced training is out there waiting for you when you decide you're ready to learn some new tricks.

Geared primarily toward un*trained* riders, the MSF Experienced Rider Course (ERC) is still a great way to blow out the winter cobwebs with some time on a parking lot and a couple of instructors for feedback. A BRC-trained and well-read rider won't find much new information in the concepts or exercises, but a rider at that level also understands the value of getting back to the basics and practicing important techniques like low-speed balance and control, cornering, braking, and swerving—exactly what the ERC does. The ERC is fairly cheap and only takes about five hours, which makes it a perfect annual tradition: Start every riding season with one.

(If you want to toss your hat into a different ring, you might also consider the MSF Dirt Bike School. A fun-as-heck course for all ages, you can learn a whole basket of new skills that may come in handy on the street. Who knows? You might even develop a new obsession.)

Track Days and Schools

Hundreds of organizations use racetracks—honest-to-goodness roadracing circuits—for riders to hone their skills at a professional level. The price of admission is seldom cheap, and full-on motorcycle-specific riding gear in good condition is mandatory. Instruction varies from none to poor, some to lots. But what you get for your time, money, and effort is something impossible to get from street riding: the ability to explore your limits and the limits of your bike without the hazards of the street. At a track school, you can ride as fast or as slow as you want, as long as you follow the rules. (As in group riding, rules mean consistency, and consistency means safety.) Imagine putting your bike through its paces with no cars, no cops, no gravelly corners, no deer, and no pedestrians to find a way to wreck your day.

A quick web search will turn up more track day events and track schools than you can possibly attend in a lifetime. You'll find there are three different types of track days: open track, controlled riding, and track school. In an open track day, they pretty much unlock the gate and give you a cheap way to get your rocks off in a relatively safe place. These organizations believe that riding your own ride, at your own pace, and learning exactly what you want to learn, are the priorities. Controlled track day organizations like the Northeast Sport Bike Association (NESBA) still require you to be responsible for yourself and you still get cheap thrills, but you also have some discipline—exactly what real safe riding is all about. To get the most out of a controlled track event, you must also be able to follow rules. You don't have to like them, but you have to respect them for the sake of your co-riders.

Most importantly, there are track schools where you learn from someone who really knows what they're doing— legendary riders like Keith Code, Freddie Spencer, Reg Pridmore, or Mick Doohan. Some of these schools are aimed at street riders, some aimed at budding roadracers, but all are *well* worth the purchase price. By signing on with a track school, you get to explore a whole new world of riding. You'll get a mind-boggling new set of thrills like wide-open sixth-gear speeds, braking from 100-plus down to 40 miles per hour, and cornering at supralegal speeds with your peg feeler, boot, and knee scraping asphalt. And you'll leave with the knowledge and tools that will bump your street riding ability up a double notch. It's not uncommon for sportbike riders to try a track day, realize what they've been "missing," run out and buy a track-only bike, and try their hand at amateur racing.

Most importantly, there are track schools where you learn from someone who really knows what they're doing—legendary riders like Keith Code, Freddie Spencer, Reg Pridmore, or Mick Doohan.

Probably the most widely known track school in the world, the California Superbike School has been broadening riders' horizons worldwide since 1980. If you want to learn from somebody, learn from a seasoned pro who knows how to teach. Luca Babini

Big Secret Number 7: Riding the Wave

Deep in the conscience of the motorcycle community, there's this irrepressible urge to raise your left arm, move your left hand back and forth, to and fro, or up and down, and commit some sort of outwardly friendly maneuver in the direction of an oncoming motorcyclist. What's really great about this urge is that you almost always get a similar gesture "right back atcha." This is the motorbike wave.

It comes in many forms: a subtle glance, quick nod, gloved-palm flashback, gotcha-pointed finger, howdy-peace sign, rock-and-roll devil fingers, down-low wrist-flipper, and sometimes, the granddaddy of all waves, the "both-hands-in-the-air-roller-coaster-Homer-Simpson-woo-hoo!" wave. Riders do this because they're out having fun on a vehicle only 1 in 10 people know how to ride—and they've just seen another 1-in-10 person. There's a bond there, a secret you share, and you can't help but acknowledge it with a little flash of greeting. In a great big world where everyone's going their millions of different ways, you and that other person have something in common—more in common than you do with most of your acquaintances.

Half the riders out there will shoot you one without being prompted, and you'll instinctively return the wave, completing the happy electric circuit. If you wave first, you'll probably get a return gesture three times out of four. Why don't they always wave back? Hard to say. Most likely, they're focused on the road or a particular hazard. (You don't have to be looking at someone to wave at them, you know!) They may be holding on for dear life (a nod would still be acceptable). They could be lost in thought (not the best time or place) or fiddling with something on their bike (what's so important down there?) and simply didn't see you. It's usually something like that.

However, there's always the chance that they may not actually be riders. Maybe they're squids or posers who aren't real motorcyclists and don't understand what riding is all really about, so they haven't developed the return-wave instinct. They're simply *not riders* so they don't *get it.* On rare occasions, it'll be worse than that: an elitist jackass who thinks that motorcycling is only about the bike or the protective gear (or lack thereof), ignoring the rider, the riding, and the road. Since you don't ride the way he or she does, you therefore have nothing in common.

(In those cases, you're better off without the wave.)

Half the riders out there will shoot you one without being prompted, and you'll instinctively return the wave, completing the happy electric circuit.

Squid: A motorcyclist, usually an 18- to 24-year-old male (but not always!) with a really fast sportbike but no knowledge of or respect for what it can do. Possibly a shortened version of the term "SQUashed kID."

Getting in Deep

By this time you're an accomplished rider, and your love for motorcycling is bursting at the seams. You can't help but start to give back to the sport that's brought you so much joy for so long.

There is a clear evolutionary ladder for motorcyclists. Feeding at the bottom, primitive and one-dimensional, we have the posers and the squids. They only care about motorcycling inasmuch as it helps them complete their self-image or attract mates. They usually ditch the bike for a safer pastime when they have to make room for a baby stroller in the garage, or when they crash it and the cost of a mistake exceeds their enthusiasm for turning heads.

Next there are riders—former posers or future enthusiasts—who use the bike for entertainment. These riders give some thought to what they do and show an interest in improving their quality of riding, but have not yet signed on to full motorcycle ownership. These weekend warriors think riding's fun and are willing to throw money at it to make it even more fun, but their riding is generally limited to summer months, sunny days, weekends, and evenings. Their bikes are usually impeccably clean. Their protective gear almost always bears the same logo as their motorcycle.

Higher up the chain come the motorcyclists. These are enthusiasts in the making who use the bike for transportation and recreation. They're relatively unfazed by weather and don't recognize a formal "motorcycle season" with beginning and ending dates. They ride whenever they can reasonably do so, and set upon books and movies about motorcycling the way a dog sets on a plate of chocolate-chip cookies.

Finally you have the enthusiasts, the ones for whom riding has become a hobby, a passion, and a lifestyle. They choose their food, shelter, and clothing based on how it fits into their motorcycling program. Their four-year-old kids know more about motorcycles than the average poser. Their garage is typically crammed with bikes, accessories, tools, and parts. They have a lot of maps, and they know how to use them.

By the time you reach enthusiast stage, your mind is consumed with all things motorcycle and you can't help but spread the word and share what you know in order to make motorcycling, as a whole, better. This means you get active among motorcycle communities, teach others to ride, and act as a mentor to less-evolved riders in your circle—or sit down and write a book about what you've learned over the years.

There is a clear evolutionary ladder for motorcyclists. Feeding at the bottom, primitive and one-dimensional, we have the posers and the squids.

Any rider who owns a rain suit is on the path to becoming a true motorcyclist. If you don't own one or can't see any reason to buy one, you're probably just a fair-weather rider.

No matter who you are or what you ride, an Internet-based group out there is probably discussing exactly the things you most want to talk about.

Motorcycle Communities

With so many riders out there, inevitably some of them come together. The enthusiastic and energetic coalesce into groups of like-minded motorcyclists to share experiences, ideas, and knowledge—and go riding.

Riding Clubs. Groups organize in all sorts of formats, but the most common are those based on a type of riding (Honda Sport Touring Association, Central Roadracing Association), make of motorcycle (Harley Owners Group, BMW Owners of America), and model-specific (Gold Wing Road Riders Association, Concours Owners Group, et al). Larger national groups sometimes break out into geographically centered chapters, but not always. Newer riders join these organizations and meet more experienced riders from whom to learn. Experienced riders in these organizations help mentor newer riders to make their group, and motorcycling in general, better and safer.

The typical requirement to be accepted into one of these groups is a membership fee, usually $75 a year or less. With that, you'll usually get a newsletter or magazine focused on your type of riding, make, or model. You'll also receive information on organized rides and events, discounts at various businesses, and pins, patches, or stickers to help you identify yourself to other riders in the group. There's nothing like a big, happy smiley-face on the back of your jacket to show you're a proud member of the "Yellow Faces of Motorcycle Madness in Upstate New York Club."

Internet Forums. On the more modern side of the motorcycle community are the online forums. Essentially moderated chat rooms, online forums allow a group of motorcyclists to share vast quantities of information from the comfort of their own homes with the click of a button. Internet forums are usually free, very narrowly focused, and have members all across the country or the world. Larger groups with enough members will sometimes divide into subforums based on

No matter if your interest in motorcycling is technical, emotional, geographical, or political; there is a group out there for you. You may find them on the road, through your dealership, or out on the Internet. They're there and when you join one, you've just tapped a new source of information and started up yet another learning curve.

location, and participants will meet up for group rides or events.

No matter who you are or what you ride, an Internet-based group out there is probably discussing exactly the things you most want to talk about. Look around and you'll find groups aptly called Friends Against Slow Travel (FAST) or Prettyboys On Sportbikes Experiencing Roadrash (POSER), or my favorite, Loudmouths Against the Use of a Good Helmet Allied with Blowhards Leading by Example (LAUGHABLE). Whether you have questions about motorcycle repair, model-specific add-ons and accessories, riding skills and techniques, or protective gear, there's always at least 1,000 people with experience in the subject, or at least an opinion. As an experienced rider, it's an easy way to help less-experienced riders past some of the bumps in the road and give them the wisdom and encouragement they need to survive.

Organizations. Serving a greater purpose in the motorcycle world are organizations like the American Motorcyclist Association, Motorcycle Riders Foundation, and American Bikers for Awareness, Training, and Education. Usually political in nature, these groups are made up of riders from

Motorcycle organizations are all about promoting motorcycling to the world, including sanctioning race events. Your membership fee goes to help ensure enthusiasts of all kinds can continue to enjoy riding for a lifetime.

You never can know it all, so you need to keep exploring for exploration's sake.

all walks of life committed to enhancing motorcycling's public image, protecting riders' rights, and lobbying against "totalitarian enactments" like helmet laws.

Even if you don't agree with some of their politics, the organizations' work overall is necessary and important to riders everywhere.

What People Say and What People Mean Number 7: "The More You Know, the Better It Gets."

Most riders have heard this mantra of the MSF, but most riders eventually reach a point where they think they know it all.

Sure, you know lots. But there's a big difference between someone saying, "I know what I like" and "I like what I know." You know lots, but you don't know *everything*. You never can know it all, so you need to keep exploring for exploration's sake. The fact is that so much knowledge is available out there, so much wisdom in every garage and every attitude and every roadside stop, so much *experience* out there, there's no limit to the amount you can learn and grow as a motorcycle rider. You only have to allow room for it in your riding philosophy.

This is your wake-up call. (As an intelligent rider, you've been doing this all along, but everybody hits the wall eventually.) Your final advice: Try something new. Even if you know you're never going to get involved in motocross racing, try taking a dirt bike course anyway. Learn to hop big logs and turn on 45-degree hills. What could it possibly hurt, and hey—it's on a motorcycle, right? Even if you know that there's no way you'd ever want to race a motorcycle, try a track day just to see what all the fuss is about. Even if you're happy with your own riding style and the results you've gotten from it, try following someone else's rules once in a while. Follow a faster rider and try to keep up, or at least try to push your boundaries a little. You just might surprise yourself with what you learn—about motorcycling, about your skills, and about yourself.

At some time in their riding careers, these coaches decided they wanted to really dig in, get involved, and do their part to make motorcycling better by making riders safer.

The Newest Rider Coach

Among motorcyclists, there's a subculture of outgoing, generous curmudgeons that dedicate a great deal of otherwise ideal riding time to teach people how to ride. Formerly labeled "instructors," these kinder, gentler "rider coaches" are the hands-on facilitators of the MSF Basic Rider Course. What these people all have in common is that they have definite and immovable opinions about motorcycling—and they're not afraid to share them. Pick any two rider coaches anywhere, stick them together in a locked room, and they'll quickly disagree about something so they can argue all afternoon, demonstrating their knowledge like peacocks attracting a mate and learning new viewpoints to assimilate into their riding system.

At some time in their riding careers, these coaches decided they wanted to really dig in, get involved, and do their part to make motorcycling better by making riders safer. If you have a particular interest in safe riding techniques or strategies, or if you're at this

stage of your development and have this nagging feeling that you're doing a lot more taking than giving, you're probably in the right frame of mind to become a rider coach.

Like motorcycling in general, becoming a rider coach is mostly about attitude. Any rider with an open mind and good motorcycle skills can learn to teach the BRC. The one real sticking point that most coaches (or instructors) have trouble with is the *outcome* of the BRC. Many, many coaches, well meaning or otherwise, dive into teaching with the idea that their students are going to emerge as competent, capable motorcyclists. For a 15-to 20-hour class, we both know that's not possible. You can't learn it all in a weekend. If you're willing to stick to the curriculum, allow students to learn by doing, and keep your mouth shut, you'll soon be churning out students who have gotten through those first 100 or so dangerous miles with all the tools they need to get out there on the street and start practicing in the real world.

When you've got the knowledge, skill, and humility to start giving back to motorcycling, the most important way you can do it is to get involved in your state program and start new riders off on the right foot.

Students can't learn it all in a weekend. If you're willing to stick to the curriculum, allow students to learn by doing, and keep your mouth shut, you'll soon be churning out students who have gotten through those first 100 or so dangerous miles.

The greatest gift you can give yourself as an experienced rider is the knowledge other experienced riders bring to your table. You never stop learning, and at this stage of the game, you'll do most of your learning interacting with other riders, whether you're teaching them or they're teaching you.

Mentoring Another Rider

By hook or crook, you'll someday find yourself in the position of teaching someone else to ride. You'd better do it. As an experienced rider you have something of a duty to share what you know. Some newer riders will ask for help, most will not, but all of them will listen carefully because deep down inside they know they should. Your job is to, initially, try to talk them *out* of it. This is peer pressure at its finest. Make them convince you that they're willing to take it seriously, and know (or think they know) what they're getting into.

When you encounter a potential or new rider and find yourself obligated to help them along, it will be up to you to take that bull by the horns and steer it in the right direction. Start by using the analogy of the iceberg to bring them up to speed on the reality of motorcycling: There's a lot more to it than meets the eye. If they want to ride, they're going to need to commit to learning it all—or else you're not going to bother with helping create a half-assed motor-cyclist (poser).

Hopefully, the potential rider has come to you before they've started riding, but that doesn't happen often. If they've already jumped in, the first step is to figure out where that rider is on the food chain. What do they like about riding? What do they wear for protective gear? Have they taken the BRC yet? What is their attitude toward the road and traffic and hazards? How many miles do they have under their belt? The answers to these questions will give you an idea of how far along that rider is on the rider development curve. Define the curve as having seven stages. Start at the lowest possible stage, the one that contains key information that the rider is missing.

Stage One: Mental Preparation. Understanding the rider's motivation will help guide you through the rest of the stages. You'll need to impart the three basic attitudes toward riding: 1. The rider is responsible for everything that happens on the road; 2. Every other driver is delib-erately trying to kill them; 3. The road is

designed to make them crash. Riders at this stage need to fully understand the Three Degrees of Separation and that their biggest risk, for at least the next couple of years, will be themselves.

Stage Two: Starting Out. Help your understudy pick out good riding gear before choosing a bike, if possible. Concentrate on finding comfortable gear that they like. If they're reluctant about the helmet, get them to at least *try* one for the first few months while they're learning, and mention the virtues of helmet use if they're someday caught out in the rain. Guide them through the bike-selection process to choose an appropriate beginner bike. Assure them that holding off on buying their dream bike now is the best approach, and that they'll learn faster and be a better rider overall by starting

When you encounter a potential or new rider and find yourself obligated to help them along, it will be up to you to take that bull by the horns and steer it in the right direction.

small. Help them do a safety check of the motorcycle and adjust the controls to fit them perfectly.

Stage Three: Getting Acquainted. If your apprentice is a bare-bones newbie, help them get a feel for the controls and riding while in the garage with the bike turned off. Don't be tempted to take them out riding before they've completed the BRC, but it's a good idea to take them out as passengers on your bike so they can get a feel for what the proper technique feels like. If they've already fumbled their way through learning to operate the bike, have them show you what they know. Ride with them and watch their basic riding ability in smooth starts and stops, the slow-roll-look-press cornering method, upshifting and accelerating, and slowing and downshifting.

Stage Four: Skill Development. Get them to take the BRC or an ERC. Take it with them if you have to. *No rider should go past Stage Four without training.* Once they've completed the course and have their permit or license in hand, help them develop a training circuit of low-speed, familiar roads and ride it with them when you can. Teach them to visualize the route before they ride it. Make an effort to demonstrate the 30–60 seconds of concentration you need before you swing that leg over the bike. Work on different skills on different days: stopping, sharp turns, shifting, faster turns, cornering technique, emergency braking, swerving, and low speed maneuvers like U-turns. Mix it up and try to help keep it fun. Spend at least a couple of weeks and a few hundred miles running them through these drills before you start venturing out.

All the decisions a rider makes at this stage will be much better with a mentor. Take the time to help your new rider understand how to select a bike and gear based on its intended use.

Help your understudy pick out good riding gear before choosing a bike. Concentrate on finding comfortable gear that they like. If they're reluctant about the helmet, get them to at least try one for the first few months while they're learning.

Stage Five: Becoming Familiar. At this point your charge will be chomping at the bit to get out and do some real riding. They're probably going to be feeling that they know enough to handle anything. (They're closer, but they're not there yet.) Help them work up to different types of roads and traffic gradually, starting with what they know best and venturing away from the safety of that familiarity only a little at a time. Make sure they understand what Motorcyclist Information Overload is and how to reduce or eliminate it. It's also important that they realize at this stage the relationships between speed and risk and speed and predictability.

An average rider should be able to achieve stage five in their first year of riding.

Stage Six: Better, Smarter. Now your newbie rider is probably approaching the level of novice, and they're going to be pretty comfortable operating the bike without thinking—and now suddenly able to absorb a lot of new information. It's time to really explore the tips and

techniques for safe riding in all sorts of conditions: busy intersections, freeways, country roads, heavy traffic, night riding, bad weather, and rush-hour commuter traffic. You can spend a whole year on this stage alone.

Stage Seven: Enthusiast Involvement. You've now created another motorcyclist. You can help them with the fun stuff that comes at this level: picking out another bike and selling their training bike. You can teach them to carry passengers—by offering to be their first passenger and giving them tips along the way. They'll be ready to try a group ride by this time, and you should consider getting out and taking an ERC or doing a track day or track school together. Most importantly, you'll need to advise your apprentice that he or she is now an informed, grown-up motorcyclist, and they are no longer only responsible for themselves. They are responsible to give back to motorcycling and to help other riders gain the knowl-

It's also important that they realize at this stage the relationships between speed and risk and speed and predictability.

Photo by Kevin Wing. Courtesy *Motorcycle Cruiser*.

Ride along and watch while your pupil is on the training circuit. Self evaluation is great for any rider, but nothing compares to informed and honest feedback on riding style and technique.

Most importantly, you'll need to advise your apprentice that he or she is now an informed, grown-up motorcyclist. They are responsible to give back to motorcycling and to help other riders gain the knowledge and skills they need to continue to make motorcycling the great adventure, sport, passion, and obsession that it is.

edge and skills they need to continue to make motorcycling the great adventure, sport, passion, and obsession that it is.

Recommended Reading:

The Pace by Nick Ienatsch—An article, the best of its kind, written about group riding. Find it, read it, and abide by it. Entire organizations are built around the type of riding described by *The Pace*.

Ride Hard, Ride Smart by Pat Hahn— For the rider who knows it all and is looking to find new ways to ride safer. Assuming you have learned everything contained in this book and know it by heart, and assuming you've also read all the "recommended reading" entries at the end of each chapter, Pat Hahn's first book is a way to start over again as a beginner—but on a much, much higher level.

INDEX

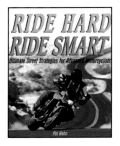

Ride Hard, Ride Smart
ISBN: 0-7603-1760-7

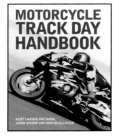

Motorcycle Track Day Handbook
ISBN: 0-7603-1761-5

Total Control
ISBN: 0-7603-1403-9

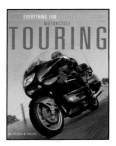

Motorcycle Touring: Everything You Need to Know
ISBN: 0-7603-2035-7

101 Harley-Davidson Twin Cam Performance Projects
ISBN: 0-7603-1639-2

101 Sportbike Performance Projects
ISBN: 0-7603-1331-8

Ultimate Garage Handbook
ISBN: 0-7603-1640-6

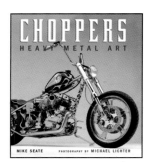

Choppers: Heavy Metal Art
ISBN: 0-7603-2053-5

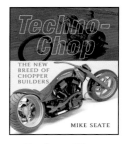

Techno-Chop: The New Breed of Chopper Builders
ISBN: 0-7603-2116-7